One who is samurai must, before all things, keep constantly in mind,

by day and by night....that he has to die.

– Daidoji Yuzan, a 16th century military advisor

Samurai

The Code of the Warrior

男道土鳳金

雷正庄九ゟ

Samurai
The Code of the Warrior

Thomas Louis and Tommy Ito

STERLING

New York / London
www.sterlingpublishing.com

Library of Congress Cataloging-in-Publication Data Available

1 2 3 4 5 6 7 8 9 10

Published in 2008 by Sterling Publishing Co., Inc.
387 Park Avenue South, New York, NY 10016

© 2006 JW Cappelens forlag under license from Gusto Company AS
Written by Thomas Louis and Tommy Ito
Original concept by Gusto Company
Designed by Allen Boe
Illustrations, Corbis and AnnDréa Boe

Distributed in Canada by Sterling Publishing
c/o Canadian Manda Group, 165 Dufferin Street
Toronto, Ontario, Canada M6K 3h6

For information about custom editions, special sales, premium and corporate purchases,
please contact Sterling Special Sales Department at 800-805-5489 or specialsales@
sterlingpub.com

Manufactured in China

Sterling ISBN: 978-1-4027-6312-0

花鳥風月内

月

桜已濡と揚俵養

Contents

Introduction

Japanese culture is unique, and its evolution has often been attributed to Japan's development as an island nation. The nation's history is a story of centuries of civil war, rivalries between clans, occasional invasions from abroad, and even brief attempts to subjugate neighbors.

Against this backdrop of ceaseless wrangling, one group—the samurai— emerged as a supreme military and political ruling class to dominate old Japan for many centuries. The story of the samurai warrior charts the rise and fall of the most skilled and courageous group of elite combatants the world has ever seen. Many of these fearsome fighters achieved legendary status and their ethos still exerts a powerful influence on Japan's national spirit.

This book examines the samurai's place in Japan's history, from the earliest island settlers to the abolition of the samurai in the late nineteenth century. It investigates what life was like for the samurai, from infancy to adulthood, whether at peace, on campaign, or in the heat of battle. What they ate and drank, where they lived, how they filled their leisure time, and how they expressed their philosophical and religious beliefs are examined in fascinating detail.

Although the samurai are well known for their use of the sword, they began as skilled mounted archers, and used a variety of weapons, including longbows, spears, and firearms. All of their weapons, armor, costumes, heraldry, and military strategies are explained in a straightforward and far-reaching analysis that brings their complex development to life.

Scattered throughout the book are detailed biographies of some of the most influential and famous samurai, showcasing their exploits, and their legacy.

What emerges is a picture of a multifaceted and sophisticated force, whose adherents valued tradition over individualism, death above dishonor, and loyalty over self-interest, but who nevertheless sought to distinguish themselves in a brutal and bloodthirsty arena where the macabre collection of enemy heads was considered a noble and prestigious priority.

Two of the most remarkable aspects of samurai culture are *bushido*, a strict philosophy which places absolute loyalty to the master above all else, and *seppuku*—ritual suicide, performed in preference to dishonor.

This book seeks to understand the actions and thoughts of these remarkable men, who have been a source of mystery and wonder to Westerners for centuries, and who still fascinate us today.

Timeline

1156	Hogen Rebellion
1160	Heiji Rebellion
1180	First battle of Uji; Gempei War begins
1184	Battle of Yashima
1185	Gempei War ends
1192	Shogunate created by Minamoto Yoritomo
1199	Death of Minamoto Yoritomo
1219	Shokyu Rebellion
1274	First Mongol invasion of Japan
1281	Second Mongol invasion of Japan
1318	Revolt of Go-Daigo
1331	Siege of Akasaka
1333	Go-Daigo returns from exile to renew revolt; Hojo family commit mass *seppuku* (ritual suicide)
1336	Battle of Minatogawa; start of Nanbokucho Wars
1348	Battle of Shijo Nawate
1467	Onin War begins
1477	Onin War ends

1543	Arrival of Europeans in Japan
1553-64	Five battles of Kawanakajima
1560	Imagawa Yoshimoto marches on Kyoto, but defeated by Oda Nobunaga
1570	Battle of Anegawa
1575	Battle of Nagashino
1588	"Sword Hunt" bans peasantry from bearing arms
1591	Separation Edict separates the military from agricultural laborers
1592	First invasion of Korea
1597	Second invasion of Korea
1600	Battle of Sekigahara
1603	Tokugawa shogunate established at Edo (Tokyo)
1614-15	Siege of Osaka Castle

1635	*Sankin kotai* ("alternate attendance system") formalized
1637	Shimabara Rebellion
1639	Closed Country Edict
1650	Law passed forbidding dueling between samurai
1702	The Forty-seven Ronin of Ako kill Kira Yoshinaka
1864-68	Meiji Restoration
1867	Shogunate officially ends
1868	Edo renamed Tokyo and replaces Kyoto as the official capital (even though Edo had been the de facto capital since 1603)
1877	Satsuma Rebellion

CHAPTER 1

Rise and Fall of the Samurai

Situated in the Pacific Ocean, off the coast of eastern Asia, Japan is made up of four main mountainous islands (Honshu, Shikoku, Kyushu, and Hokkaido) and numerous smaller ones. It has always had close cultural links with nearby Korea and China through trade and war.

Japan was inhabited for thousands of years before the concept of the "samurai" was used to refer to a military warrior. In fact, archaeological evidence places humans in Japan as long as 100,000 years ago. Over many eons two distinct cultures emerged. The first was the Jomon people who were hunter-gatherers (their name means "rope pattern," referring to the pattern on their pottery). The other was the Yayoi who are more closely identified with the modern Japanese, because they cultivated rice and were more technically advanced than the Jomon.

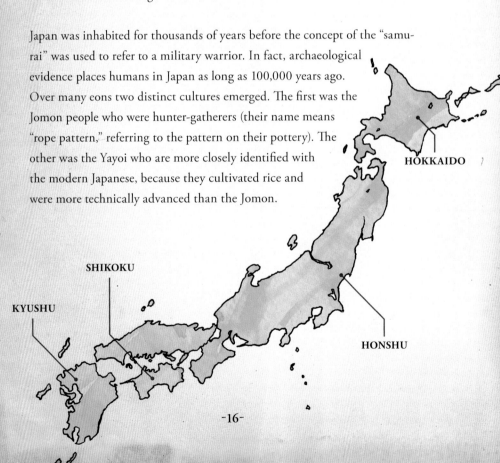

HOKKAIDO

SHIKOKU

KYUSHU

HONSHU

The earliest records of Japanese warfare kept by contemporary Chinese dynasties show that, in early times, Japan was involved in expeditionary wars with the three neighboring kingdoms in Korea: Paekche, Koguryo, and Silla.

These early Japanese expeditions involved men on foot using bows, swords, and spears; they were trampled by Korean cavalry, and as a result a century later horses were being ridden in Japan. Between the fourth and seventh centuries there were several rival clans, from which the Yamato clan emerged victorious to become the ancestors to the Japanese emperors of later generations. These early rulers were buried in huge earthen tombs, called *kofun*, along with hoards of weapons, bronze mirrors, and jewels. Many of these tombs still exist and are impressive in both their size and design.

There were close trading links between Japan and the rest of Asia, and articles found inside some of the tombs indicate that, by the fourth century A.D., Japan had a settlement in Korea called Mimana, administered by the Yamato clan.

Some historians believe that the victorious Yamato clan came from Korea, bringing mounted warfare with them, whereas Japanese creation myths show the opposite: Japanese cavalry defeating the Koreans.

Whatever its origin, this relationship between Korea and Japan was very important in shaping Japan's history and religion. Buddhism came to Japan from Korea. Until then, the dominant religion in Japan was polytheistic Shintoism, "the Way of the Gods," which concerned itself with ancient creation myths and the worship of the thousands of different *kami* ("gods") which govern nature. Buddhism reached Japan in A.D. 538 when the Korean king made a gift of a single Buddha. Buddhism was quickly embraced by Japanese rulers, who used its hierarchical system to unify the country and create an equally hierarchical political system. In A.D. 593 it was declared the state religion of Japan.

THE TAIKA REFORMS

The Yamato clan was sufficiently dominant that, in A.D. 645, they issued edicts called the Taika reforms, which placed the whole of Japan under the rule of a single emperor, thereby founding the Japanese imperial system and centralized government. In the edicts, the emperor justified his position with this declaration:

"In Heaven there are not two suns: in a country there are not two rulers.
It is therefore the Emperor alone who is supreme over all the Empire, and
who has a right to the services of the myriad people . . . the Emperors take
Heaven as their [hierarchical] model in ruling the World."

The reforms also established Japan's first capital city at Nara in A.D. 710, and for a while society was stable and peaceful. Buddhist art flourished and any uprisings from rival clans were easily dealt with. In A.D. 743 the world-famous Todaiji temple was started. Inside was a colossal brass Buddha that is forty-nine feet tall—the largest in the world.

Although clans were important up until the eighth century, the organizational structure developed into a feudal system thereafter. As historian Karl Friday explains:

"'Clan' has . . . little meaning at all in Japanese history after the 8th
century or so. The main familial unit for warriors and non-warriors
alike was the household. Kinship ties, both real and fictitious, were
exploited in various ways by would-be warlords attempting to establish
'feudal' (for lack of a better word) control over large areas of lands
and peoples, but the bonds that were formed were actually based on
financial and military dependency, not kinship."

THE RISE OF THE MOUNTED WARRIOR

It is a mistake to assume that the samurai first appeared in the twelfth century, simply because that is when they enter written records. Japan had a military tradition that stretched back for hundreds of years, so the emergence of the samurai was the result of a long and continuous development.

In A.D. 702, military reforms resulted in the Taiho system, which created a large army of conscripted peasants. This largely infantry-based army protected the imperial capital of Nara and the imperial fortress of Kyushu. Each conscript soldier served in his regiment for part of the year and tended the fields the rest of the time. He was equipped with a bow, arrows, and a pair of swords. The regiments were controlled by elite mounted archers—forerunners of the samurai.

Beneath the emperor were landowners, followed by the peasant farmers. The army of conscripted peasants wasn't very effective at suppressing rebellions, so the government began giving permission to the landowners to keep the peace. They employed elite mounted warriors who later developed into a class of their own: the samurai.

芳年武者无類

畠山
重忠

FIGHTING THE EMISHI

The northeastern part of Japan was inhabited by a group of people who were referred to by the Nara court as the *emishi*, a derogatory term which translates roughly as "barbarian." During the seventh and eighth centuries, the Nara court made several attempts to conquer these inhabitants. They were partially successful but there were several major uprisings, culminating in a major revolt in A.D. 774. The conscripted Japanese army, led by elite mounted archers, were defeated by the highly mobile *emishi* who used light armor, guerrilla tactics, and curved blades—features that were later adopted by the samurai.

Finally, in A.D. 796, the Nara court subdued the *emishi*, and the court's leader was given the title of *Sei-i-tai* shogun ("Great Barbarian-Subduing General"), a name that was later used for the leader of the samurai.

THE END OF CONSCRIPTION

After the conflict with the *emishi*, the Nara court eventually abolished the conscription system and looked to other ways of maintaining military dominance.

In A.D. 792, a new system was established: the recruitment of permanent officers called *kondei* ("strong youth") from the young sons of the landowner class. Each *kondei* was mounted, wore armor, used a bow and sword, and was supported by two grooms who were also foot soldiers.

The samurai emerged as a result of the devolvement of political power. The *kondei* were supposed to be the elite military arm of the government. They were mounted archers who passed their wealth and military traditions to their sons, but they did not have political power, and their services were often called upon by rival district landowners to settle disputes.

During the ninth century there was great civil unrest caused by plagues and famines, as well as great resentment against centralized government. The government had to devolve military power even further to the landowners, so that provincial governors had even greater scope to maintain their own private armies of elite horsemen and deal with civil unrest at a local level.

The word "samurai" began to be used to describe these elite fighters. Samurai means "those who serve," and expresses their loyalty to these warriors' lords. This loyalty, along with a system of conduct, developed into a formalized honor code which became known as *bushido*: "the Way of the Warrior" (*see page 68*).

The word "samurai" also acquired aristocratic and hereditary connotations. Initially, any peasant could rise through the ranks to become an elite fighter; later, only those born into the samurai class could become samurai.

By the eleventh century the pedigree of a samurai was paramount. A warrior could not take up a bow in the name of defending the emperor unless he could prove that he belonged to a noble lineage of samurai. Before a fight, samurai would recite a long list of their ancestors, showing off their pedigree to their opponents. Military distinction meant nothing without a bloodline. For example, in 1028, Fujiwara Norimoto was vilified for being "not of warrior blood," despite his military achievements.

TAIRA AND MINAMOTO

With their samurai armies, the landowners became stronger and richer and acquired vast territories through military conquest. These noble families joined together to form clans, and by the eleventh century there were two dominant clans: the Taira and the Minamoto. The former had put down rebellions in the north and east, while the latter had distinguished themselves by protecting trade routes and fighting pirates. When civil war broke out between these two clans, Japan entered the Age of the Sword.

By now Kyoto was the capital city, and the Hogen Rebellion of 1156 saw both families fighting over the imperial throne. The Taira won a subsequent uprising in 1160, called the Heiji Rebellion, and nearly wiped out the Minamoto clan. But the Minamoto clan regrouped, and the two clans fought again at the battle of Uji, which was the first battle of the Gempei War.

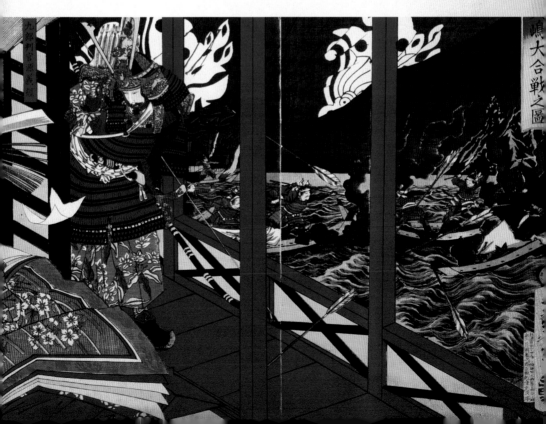

THE GEMPEI WAR

The Gempei War, fought between 1180 and 1185, was an important milestone in samurai history. It is named for the combination of the Chinese version of the names of Minamoto (Gen) and Taira (Hei).

The exploits and battles of the Gempei War set the standard for distinction that successive samurai tried to emulate. As samurai scholar Stephen Turnbull points out, "Nearly all the factors that were to become indelible parts of samurai culture have a reference point somewhere within the Gempei War. Prowess at archery and hand-to-hand fighting, the juxtaposition of art, poetry and violence, undying loyalty to one's lord and the tremendous tradition of ritual suicide, all have key passages and proof texts in the tales of the Gempei War."

Another important consequence of the Gempei War was the creation of the shogunate by Minamoto Yoritomo in 1192. This effectively meant that, while the emperor maintained his godlike status and religious power, effective political power now came under the permanent control of a military dictator—the shogun. The title was hereditary, passed down within the Minamoto family of samurai. The Minamoto family did not hold onto power for long. Yoritomo died seven years later and within two more generations his family was overthrown by the Hojo clan. However, the shogunate itself continued off and on until the second half of the nineteenth century.

Minamoto Yoritomo had been an effective politician, but a cold leader, and it is his brother, Minamoto Yoshitsune (*see page 186*), who is seen as the ideal of a samurai warrior.

THE MONGOL INVASIONS

In the thirteenth century, the biggest challenge the samurai faced was from the Mongols who, under the command of Genghis Khan, had amassed a vast empire stretching from Asia to Eastern Europe.

The first Mongol invasion took place in 1274 and the Mongols' "dishonorable" fighting methods were a shock to the samurai. The Mongols slaughtered women and children, and they were prepared to use any method to win. They also used a different archery tactic—firing a swarm of arrows at once, rather than picking off individuals at long range with single shots. However, the samurai fought bravely and forced them to retreat.

In 1281, the Mongols invaded again, but the samurai's heroism was aided by a fortuitous storm that destroyed the Mongol fleet. The "divine winds" that whipped up the storm are best known by the descriptive word *kamikaze*.

The Mongol invasions provided another milestone for heroic deeds of samurai bravery and conduct, and although it would be six centuries before a foreign power attempted to invade Japan again, the civil conflict within Japan continued with the Nanbokucho Wars.

THE NANBOKUCHO WARS

In 1318, the Emperor Go-Daigo challenged the reigning Hojo *shikken* ("regency"), and the resulting conflict was the Nanbokucho Wars, or "Wars Between the Courts."

When the Hojo sent an army from Kamakura, Go-Daigo, who had already gained the support of the warrior monks, escaped from Kyoto and went to the Todaiji in Nara, and then to Kasagi mountain, taking the imperial crown jewels with him. When the Hojo were unable to negotiate with Go-Daigo, they made another member of their family emperor in Go-Daigo's absence.

Kusunoki Masashige fought for Go-Daigo from a mountain castle called Akasaka, which fell to siege in 1331. Kusunoki and Go-Daigo's son escaped, while Go-Daigo was captured and exiled to the island of Oki. Then, Kusunoki established himself in the mountains at Chihaya where he held off the Hojo forces using guerrilla tactics until Go-Daigo returned from exile in 1333. The Hojo sent one of their leading samurai generals, Ashikaga Takauji, to defeat him. However, instead of carrying out his orders, Ashikaga switched his allegiance to Go-Daigo and attacked the Hojo's Kyoto headquarters at Rokuhara, capturing the city. On hearing the news, many of the Hojo samurai who were besieging Kusunoki also switched sides.

After their defeat, the Hojo family and their close retainers committed mass *seppuku* ("suicide"). Some of the samurai wrote poems before dying and this death-poem tradition was adopted by subsequent generations of samurai. A warrior monk named Fuonji Shinnin became famous by writing his death poem on a temple pillar with his own blood. The close family members committed mass suicide in a cave behind the Toshoji temple, which is today a site of pilgrimage.

However, turncoat samurai Ashikaga Takauji's loyalty to Go-Daigo was short-lived. When the emperor failed to reward him with the shogunate, he revolted. Go-Daigo swiftly defeated Ashikaga's army and drove him to the southern Japanese island of Kyushu, where Ashikaga regrouped and advanced on Kyoto by sea in 1336.

Kusunoki Masashige (*see page 184*) recommended that the emperor once again retreat to the mountains and fight a guerrilla war, but Go-Daigo refused and ordered him to fight him in direct battle. Kusunoki knew that this was tactical suicide, but with unquestioning loyalty he led his troops into the disastrous battle of Minatogawa, at the present-day city of Kobe. As expected, Kusunoki was defeated and committed ritual suicide, establishing himself in the panthe-on of exemplary samurai heroes for his absolute devotion to his lord.

THE ONIN WAR

The fifteenth century is characterized by many minor debacles between power-ful samurai families, culminating in the disastrous Onin War fought between 1467 and 1477. Its legacy was the destruction of Kyoto, the humiliation of the shogun, Ashikaga Yoshimasa, and a period of Japanese history known as the *Sengoku Jidai*—the "Period of Warring States"—which lasted for the next 150 years and saw many developments in samurai autonomy, weaponry, and tactics.

It was during this period that the leaders of the fighting clans and families started referring to themselves as *daimyo* ("great names," or "feudal lords"), and their heroic exploits ushered in a golden age of samurai glory not seen since the Gempei War.

Uesugi Kenshin versus Takeda Shingen

The most famous conflicts in samurai history are the five battles fought at Kawanakajima between two of Japan's greatest samurai warlords, Uesugi Kenshin and Takeda Shingen. Both men were descended from important samurai families and were skilled tacticians, the epitome of the warrior *daimyo* from the Warring States period.

Kawanakajima is a large, flat valley deep in the mountains, and the battles took place there between 1553 and 1564. The most famous is the fourth battle of Kawanakajima, which was fought on September 10, 1561. Casualties were high, with 25,000 killed. The percentage of casualties on both sides was greater than in any other battle in the Sengoku period: Takeda lost sixty-three percent of his men and Uesugi lost seventy-two percent.

In September of 1561, Uesugi Kenshin left his fortress of Kasugayama with an army of 18,000 men and marched to a mountain vantage point close to Shingen's Kaizu castle, overlooking Kawanakajima. However, this castle was guarded by only 150 men; the bulk of Shingen's force was eighty miles away at Kofu. The retainers at Kaizu used a line of signal fires to warn Shingen, who soon arrived at Kawanakajima with 20,000 men.

One of Shingen's generals, Kosaka Danjo Masanobu, led 8,000 men up the slopes of the mountain for a night ambush, intending to drive Uesugi from the mountain into the valley, where Shingen was waiting with his army. However, Uesugi pre-empted their strike by marching down the mountain at the same time. At dawn the following morning, the armies of Uesugi and Shingen squared off across the valley.

Uesugi's army attacked in waves and dominated the battle. Finally, Uesugi reached Takeda's command post and attacked him. The fight is one of the most famous in Japanese history. Takeda, taken by surprise, defended himself with his *tessen* ("battle fan") until one of his retainers wounded Uesugi's horse with a spear and drove him away.

Meanwhile, after reaching the top of the mountain and finding it empty, Masanobu and his men raced down again to form a pincer attack against Uesugi, saving the day for Takeda and claiming victory.

IMAGAWA YOSHIMOTO AND ODA NOBUNAGA

With Takeda and Uesugi greatly weakened, there was a power vacuum in Kyoto, while sporadic minor rebellions broke out between rival clans throughout Japan. But none of them were powerful enough to risk marching on the capital to claim the throne, since neighboring clans would be quick to claim the territory they had left behind. Finally, in 1560 a lord named Imagawa Yoshimoto staked his claim and marched on Kyoto. However, he first had to conquer Owari province which lay between him and the capital. It was ruled by a minor *daimyo* named Oda Nobunaga, whose army was outnumbered by Yoshimoto's twelve to one. After a surprise counterattack during a thunderstorm, Yoshimoto was killed and Oda Nobunaga achieved one of the most unlikely victories in Japanese history. His success quickly attracted the support of other samurai families, and in 1568 it was his turn to march on Kyoto, where he deposed the shogun and became regent.

Oda Nobunaga then consolidated his position at the battles of Anegawa (1570) and Nagashino (1575), where he defeated the powerful Takeda by creating a brand new samurai tactic: his foot soldiers fired disciplined volleys from 3,000 arquebuses (*see page 149*) to break up Takeda's cavalry charge.

Despite his tactical genius, in 1582 Oda Nobunaga died when one of his own generals, Akechi Mitsuhide, attacked his castle. One of Nobunaga's most trusted samurai, Toyotomi Hideyoshi, who had risen through the ranks from *ashigaru* ("foot soldier"), immediately rushed to Kyoto and quashed the coup at the battles of Yamazaki and Shizugatake.

THE SWORD HUNT AND SEPARATION EDICT

In 1588, Hideyoshi enacted a decree banning the peasantry from bearing arms. During the ensuing "Sword Hunt" all weapons were confiscated from the peasantry, and from then on only the samurai class and the *daimyo* armies were allowed to carry weapons. The peasants were told that their weapons would be melted down and used to make an image of the Buddha, but most of them were passed to the *daimyo* and stored for future campaigns.

Three years later the Separation Edict separated the military from agricultural laborers. No samurai was allowed to work on the land, and no peasant farmer was allowed to fight like a samurai. Hideyoshi destroyed the very system that had allowed him to rise through the ranks from lowly peasant to general. From that point on, only those born into samurai families could wield a sword, spear, or firearm.

The peasants' loss was the foot-soldiers' gain—the *ashigaru* now became full-time professional soldiers and members of the samurai class. They were, albeit, inferior ones, looked down on by high-ranking mounted samurai.

THE KOREAN WAR

Hideyoshi became Japan's great unifier, succeeding in creating many allies from those he conquered, rather than decimating them, so that within a decade he had united the whole of Japan. However, in the 1590s, with his sights set on the conquest of China, he attacked Korea, but was driven back by a Chinese invasion and the Korean navy.

The first invasion in 1592 began well, and Hideyoshi's samurai captured Seoul within three weeks of their arrival in Korea. They had attacked the main port of Pusan with devastating cruelty, savagely decimating the civilians. They won the battle of Sangju, and then encircled the army of Sin Rip at the important fortress of Ch'ungju. When they realized they were beaten, the Koreans rode into the river and drowned.

Then the tide of battle turned. The Japanese were delayed at the Imjin river and although they won the subsequent battle of Pyokje, the Koreans finally pressed the Japanese back to Seoul, where they wore them down with guerrilla tactics. In August 1592, a Japanese garrison at Ch'ungju was beaten by a guerrilla army which included Buddhist monks.

Under Admiral Yi Sun-sin the Koreans gained the upper hand at sea, destroying forty-seven Japanese ships and effectively ending the invasion.

Hideyoshi launched another invasion in 1597 but failed to defeat the Koreans in their coastal fortresses. With provisions spent, the death of Hideyoshi was the excuse the Japanese needed to abandon their ill-fated conquest of Korea.

THE TOKUGAWA SHOGUNATE

Hideyoshi was succeeded by his five-year-old son, which inevitably led to a power struggle between those loyal to the young ruler and a powerful *daimyo* challenger, Tokugawa Ieyasu. This conflict culminated in the battle of Sekiga-hara in 1600, the largest battle ever fought between samurai. Tokugawa won, set up a new capital at Edo (modern-day Tokyo), and established the Tokugawa shogunate in 1603 which ruled for the next two-and-a-half centuries.

He also completed the separation of peasant and samurai, begun with the Separation Edict, by physically separating them as well: the samurai and *ashigaru* now lived in the barracks within the *daimyo's* castles, and the peasant farmers lived outside the castle walls.

The most effective part of the Tokugawa shogunate's centralized feudalism was the introduction of the *sankin kotai* ("alternate attendance system"), whereby the *daimyo* was obliged to spend one year in his provincial *yashiki* ("mansion") and the following year in his mansion at the capital, Edo. His family would remain permanently at the Edo base, but he and a prescribed number of his retainers had to march to and from his country residence every year. This financial and logistical diversion greatly reduced the threat of rebellion, especially since the families were virtual hostages at Edo while the *daimyo* were away.

MEN OF THE WAVES

The civil wars that had dominated Japanese life created a large number of wandering samurai who became known as *ronin* ("men of waves"). Defeated samurai didn't always commit suicide. Often, the *daimyo* on the losing side of a civil conflict had some of his lands reinstated in return for complete loyalty to the victor, although this wasn't always possible. With a *daimyo* dead and the lands swallowed up by the victor, the samurai who had followed him were out of a job, unless they were prepared to swear allegiance to another *daimyo*, whose recruitment would have been limited by the shogun keen to keep the *daimyo* armies from becoming a threat.

The result was that in early Tokugawa Japan there were thousands of master-less *ronin* wandering the countryside in search of work. They were often treated as outcasts, but since they now answered to no one but themselves, they grew fiercely independent. Some of them terrorized local peasants, while others were hired to protect the villagers or became bodyguards for wealthy merchants. Others taught martial arts.

THE SIEGE OF OSAKA CASTLE

Toyotomi Hideyori, the son of Hideyoshi, who had been deposed by the Tokugawa in 1600, feared that they were going to do away with him, so he took refuge in his dead father's castle at Osaka, along with 120,000 loyal *ronin*. The castle had a five-story keep, three moats, and was protected by rivers on three sides. The subsequent bloody siege lasted for nearly a year.

First Ieyasu tried to capture the castle outposts using siege towers and by tunnelling underneath the walls, but he failed, and the well-provisioned *ronin* dug in for the winter. Ieyasu resorted to trickery and bribed one of Hideyori's men. This plan failed when the traitor was beheaded before he could open the

castle gate. So Ieyasu bombarded the ladies' quarters in the castle with his siege cannons. Hideyori was pressured into a peace agreement, which conceded to Ieyasu the right to fill in the outer moat of the castle, in return for calling off his army. Ieyasu called off his men and ordered them to dismantle the outer wall and use the stones to fill in the outer moat; instead, they "misunderstood" his orders and filled in two moats, dramatically reducing the castle's defenses, while Ieyasu pretended it was an innocent mistake.

The siege ended the following July in a bloody battle at Tennoji, and the heads of thousands of defeated Hideyori *ronin* were impaled on spikes for miles between Osaka and Kyoto as a warning to others.

THE SHIMABARA REBELLION

It would be another twenty years before the Tokugawa were challenged again.
By 1637, the peasants had endured years of brutal treatment from the *daimyo*,
and when they revolted, they were joined by thousands of *ronin* to form a rebel
army. Once again they were defeated and the Tokugawa didn't face another
serious challenge for 200 years.

During this time a few *ronin* achieved legendary status by becoming the "wandering swordsmen" of Japan, traveling the country on *musha shugyo* ("warrior

pilgrimages"), challenging other samurai to duels, and seeking Zen enlighten-ment. The most famous of these was Miyamoto Musashi (*see page 154*), who has been immortalized in numerous plays, books, and movies.

Other samurai left Japan and went abroad to seek employment. Some became merchants, others pirates and mercenaries. The most famous of these samurai mercenaries was Yamada Nagamasa, who served the King of Siam (modern-day Thailand), married a Siamese princess, and became governor of a province.

THE DECLINE OF THE SAMURAI

In 1639, the Tokugawa Shogunate issued the Closed Country Edict which ostensibly stopped all trade with the West, although trade with China and Korea continued. This act was intended to weaken potential rebel *daimyo* by severing their contact with Europe. This also put an end to samurai mercenaries venturing overseas, and during the next two centuries, with no fighting to be had at home, the development of martial arts from the martial disciplines of the Age of War was the samurai's main outlet. Most samurai were bored and without a purpose, with skills that had no outlet after 1650 when a law was passed banning dueling among them. Their skills were dulling so that by 1690 a law had to be passed to force the samurai to practice martial arts. They were a dying breed in a world where townfolk were prospering through trade and enjoying a better standard of living, while the samurai survived on a fixed stipend.

By the early eighteenth century, the samurai were spending more time engaged in arts and crafts to supplement their income than performing martial arts. According to some accounts, they even pawned their sword blades to survive, replacing them with bamboo hidden inside their sheaths.

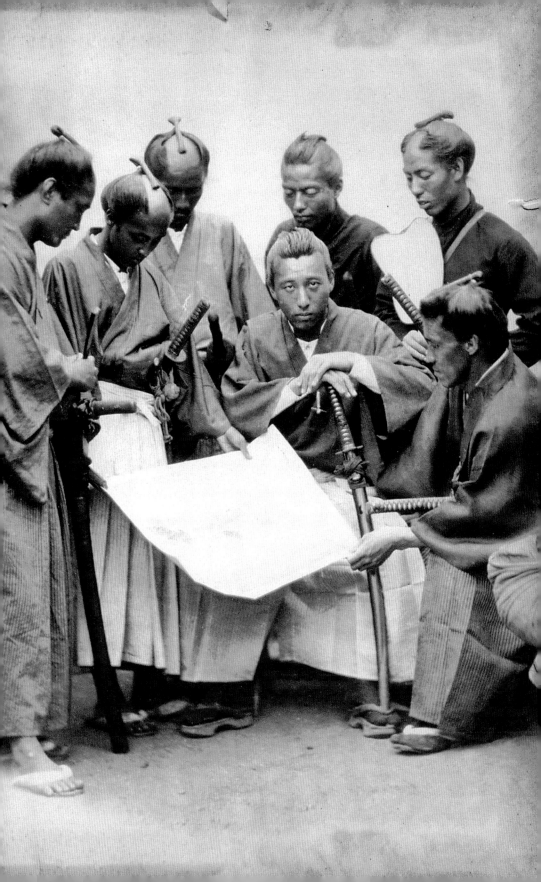

THE MEIJI RESTORATION

The era of the samurai came to an end with the Meiji Restoration (1864-1868), in which the Tokugawa shogunate was finally deposed and Japan began a process of modernization and reforging links with other countries.

The clans from the Choshu area wanted to resist influence from the Western world. The shogun announced that expulsion of all foreigners would begin in the middle of 1863, but when no action was taken, the Choshu clans started attacking foreign ships along the Shimonoseki strait and building forts along the coastline. On the appointed day, when foreigners were supposed to be expelled, only the Choshu took action, firing on a United States merchant ship, followed by a French ship two weeks later. American and French ships arrived to return fire, and the following year a fleet consisting of ships from four foreign nations attacked Japan. This crisis meant that peasants were once again armed and trained in using guns, ending the samurai's exclusive right to bear arms and fight. The samurai found themselves reduced to training peasants in the use of firearms.

In 1866, Kido Takayoshi, the Choshu leader, and Saigo Takamori, the leader of the Satsuma domain, formed an alliance and challenged the Tokugawa shogunate, restoring the emperor to power. The shogunate officially ended on November 9, 1867, when Tokugawa Yoshinobu resigned. The new emperor encouraged modernization of Japan and its army, and the samurai, stripped of their privileges, faded away with one last debacle, the failed Satsuma Rebellion of 1877 which ended with the suicide of Saigo Takamori, one of the last of the samurai.

Akamatsu
Mitsusuke

1381-1441

Akamatsu Mitsusuke was a great-grandson of Akamatsu Norimura, who is credited with gaining the family's power in the Muromachi Period. Norimura initially supported Emperor Go-Daigo in the Kemmu Restoration, but later switched his allegiance to Ashikaga. Norimura was named governor of Harima in 1336 and by the third Ashikaga shogunate, the Akamatsu controlled Harima, Bizen, and Mimasaka, and were one of four families with members on the *bakufu*'s ("shogunate's") samurai-*dokoro* ("board of retainers"). Mimasaka was added to the Akamatsu territory when the Yamana clan was defeated in 1391, resulting in the Yamana's long-running contempt toward the Akamatsu. It was a family feud that would surface generations later and gravely affect Akamatsu Mitsusuke.

In 1408, the twenty-three-year-old Ashikaga Yoshimochi became shogun, succeeding Yoshimitsu. In 1427, just a year before Ashikaga Yoshimochi's death, the unpredictable—and, according to some, unbalanced—Akamatsu Mitsusuke was serving as head of the Yamana. The shogun planned to replace Mitsusuke with Akamatsu Mochisada, rumored to be Yoshimochi's lover. Learning of the plan, and intending to thwart it, Mitsusuke left Kyoto for Mimasaka, the Yamana's former lands. Yoshimochi declared the act treasonous and ordered his army to pursue Mitsusuke. The order, however, was ignored and the shogun's retainers dissuaded him not only from pursuing Mitsusuke, but also from replacing him. Yoshimochi's change of heart created an intolerably embarrassing situation for Mochisada, who took responsibility for the political mess and

赤松満祐

committed suicide. Mitsusuke opted to withdraw for a time, becoming a monk until Yoshimochi's death in 1428.

Yoshimochi was succeeded by his brother, Yoshinori, who in 1428 became shogun at age thirty-four. In a bizarre bit of *déjà vu*, Yoshinori also plotted to oust Mitsusuke. Like his brother and predecessor, Yoshinori hatched the plot a year before his death and proposed replacing Mitsusuke with his suspected lover, Akamatsu Sadamura.

This time, Mitsusuke responded more boldly than he had twelve years earlier. When the shogun returned from a campaign against the Yuki family in the northern part of the Hitatchi province, Mitsusuke invited Yoshinori to his Kyoto home for a victory celebration. During the party, Yoshinori and other guests were being entertained by dancers in the garden when several horses got loose, causing a substantial commotion. Mitsusuke, of course, had planned the distraction and took advantage of the confusion to have Yoshinori assassinated.

News of Yoshinori's death caused outrage in Kyoto. Warriors from the Yamana, Hosokawa, and Hatakeyama families set out after three days in pursuit of Mitsusuke, but lost their resolve on the edge of the Akamatsu lands. Only Yamana Sozen and his soldiers forged on, but they were able to beat the Akamatsu and forced Mitsusuke to commit suicide. As a result, Sozen was awarded most of the Akamatsu lands including Mimasaka, which the Akamatsu had taken from the Yamana generations before.

Anayama Beisetsu
(Nobukimi)

1541-1582

The Anayama were descended from Takeda Nobutake, whose son, Yoshitake, was given Anayama in Kai Province in the mid-fourteenth century.

Anayama Beisetsu, also known as Anayama Genba no Kami Nobukimi, was the son of Anayama Nobutomo, who died in 1560; his mother was a daughter of Takeda Nobutora. Anayama was both a nephew and brother-in-law to the powerful Takeda Shingen and became one of the infamous Twenty-Four Generals.

Among his many battles, Anayama is known to have served at the fourth battle of Kawanakajima in 1561, Minowa in 1566, Odawara in 1569, and Mikatagahara in 1572. He led a large contingent at the Battle of Nagashino in 1575. Although Anayama commanded large numbers in Takeda Shingen's army, he was viewed as a mediocre general who acted as a firearms expert.

Anayama was given Ejiri Castle and land in the Suruga province after its capture in 1569, where he remained for about ten years. During that time Anayama held a noteworthy place in the Takeda hierarchy under Shingen's son Katsuyori. The relationship with Katsuyori was less than amicable, although the basis for the hard feelings between the two is unclear. One story proposes

穴山信君

that Anayama became angry with Takeda Katsuyori since he ordered Takeda Yoshinobu to commit suicide in 1567. Anayama Nobukimi had been close to Takeda Yoshinobu and blamed Katsuyori for his fall.

Perhaps as a consequence of the hard feelings toward Takeda Katsuyori, Anayama betrayed the Takedas in 1582, throwing his allegiance to Tokugawa Ieyasu. He accompanied Tokugawa to the capital region, but was forced to flee during the rebellion of Akechi Mitsuhide. Due to health problems—possibly hemorrhoids—Anayama was unable to ride. While Tokugawa Ieyasu and his troops were safely escorted out of the area by allies, Anayama was forced to take—or insisted upon taking—a different route. On the way, he was killed near the Uji River in an ambush that was likely coordinated and executed by former Takeda retainers.

Anayama Nobukimi had one son, Anayama Nobuharu, who lived only fifteen years, from 1572 to 1587, dying just five years after his father.

CHAPTER 2

Samurai Daily Life

LIFE THROUGH DEATH

The most famous and influential samurai treatise is the *Hagakure* by Yamamoto Tsunetomo. Tsunetomo was one of the closest retainers of the *daimyo* Nabeshima Mitsushige. When his master died, instead of committing suicide, as was often the custom, he asked permission to become a Buddhist monk, moved into a hermitage, and lived in seclusion. A decade later he was visited by a young samurai who spent the next seven years recording the wisdom of Yamamoto Tsunetomo in the *Hagakure*, which means "hidden leaves." Today, his utterances give us important insight into what it meant to be a samurai and how a samurai was expected to conduct himself.

In the first chapter are these words:

"The Way of the Samurai is found in death. When it comes . . . there is only the quick choice of death . . . we all want to live . . . but not having attained our aim and continuing to live is cowardice . . . If by setting one's heart right every morning and evening, one is able to live as though his body were already dead, he gains freedom in the Way."

We include this passage here because it is important to highlight that the samurai lived every day with the dual realities of death and a life well-lived. When we examine the daily life and the beliefs that shape a samurai's conduct, it is always against a backdrop of his own death.

A later passage instructs how "meditation on inevitable death should be performed daily. Every day when one's body and mind are at peace, one should meditate upon being ripped apart by arrows, rifles, spears and swords, being carried away by surging waves, being thrown into the midst of a great fire, being struck by lightning, being shaken to death by a great earthquake, falling from thousand foot cliffs, dying of disease or committing *seppuku* at the death of one's master. And every day without fail one should consider himself as dead."

Even an act as apparently simple as growing a moustache was an act of preparation for death. The *Hagakure* explains that the warriors of old grew moustaches so that, if they were killed in battle and their heads were chopped off, there could be no mistake that it belonged to a warrior and not a woman; hence "growing a moustache was one of the disciplines of a samurai so that his head would not be thrown away upon his death."

TRAINING

When not on a military campaign, a samurai would spend most of his time developing his fighting skills. He knew that the mastery of martial arts was more than just a matter of physical strength. He developed *haragei* ("mental concentration") and focused life energy called *ki*.

In order to control his energy, the samurai would perform a repetitive sequence of moves called *kata*, slowly at first to perfect the technique, then building up speed to increase their lethal power. The movements were built around attack, defense, and counterattack strategies. The sword-drilling method, called *suburi*, involved swinging the sword over and over again at an imaginary opponent.

A young samurai first learned the basic sword techniques with a real sword against an imaginary opponent. Then, two opponents would spar with practice wooden swords (*bokuto*) or edgeless swords (*habiki*). For spear training, a student used a spear with a padded end called a *tampo yari*. Fighting with practice weapons was not without its risks. The student did not wear armor, and the practice weapons could cause severe bruising and even broken limbs.

A child born into a samurai family was immersed in warrior culture from its first breath. During its birth a priest, or the baby's father, pulled a drawstring so that the twanging sound might ward off evil spirits. The future samurai was presented with a small sword talisman to wear from infancy.

At three he would begin practicing the basics of fencing with wooden swords, and at the age of five he would receive his first haircut and be presented with a real sword, a *mamorigatana*, for self-defense. The most important rite of passage for a young samurai took place between ages thirteen and sixteen, in a ceremony called *genpuku*. Here he received his first adult haircut, sword (a *wakizashi*, see page 138), and armor. He was also permitted to wear a *katana* ("sword") (*see*

page 130), but it was usually sealed into its scabbard with string to prevent it being drawn accidentally.

The front of his head would be shaved, while the long hair at the back would be oiled and bound in a ponytail. He was expected to keep the ponytail for the rest of his life; to cut it off was considered a disgrace. Having come of age he was now expected to follow his father into battle.

Samurai girls did not receive formal education, but they were expected to run their husbands' estate while they were away at war. They also received martial arts training, especially in the *yari* and *naginata*, and there are many examples of samurai women fighting alongside their husbands. The most famous samurai woman, Tomoe Gozen, lived during the Gempei Wars. She decapitated the enemy leader after he ripped her clothes, and she presented his head to her husband.

The amount of training a samurai received depended on his family's wealth. In lower-class families boys would be sent to the village school for basic education and receive samurai training from their close male relatives.

During the Age of Warring States, samurai schools were established in which a master, called a *sensei*, would teach his skills. Children from wealthy families were sent to these academies where they were schooled in literature and the arts, including the martial arts.

During the peaceful Tokugawa period this emphasis was even more important, since samurai needed these extra skills to supplement their meager stipend. This was in marked contrast to the earlier periods when constant civil war meant that, out of necessity, military training was prioritized, so that there were many illiterate samurai during periods of great conflict. Hojo Nagauji, writing in the sixteenth century, instructed his students that "when one has the least bit of spare time, he should always take out some piece of literature or something with characters on it that he has kept in his pocket, and read where no one will be looking."

At the end of the sixteenth century samurai started practicing with a *shinai*, a pole made out of light bamboo.

The later stages of training involved fighting an opponent with deadly sharp weapons. This was often combined with a technique called *tsumeru*, where a strike would be stopped a fraction of an inch before hitting its target. Miyamoto Musashi (*see page 154*) was the greatest practitioner of *tsumeru*. It is said that he was able to slice a grain of rice placed on an opponent's head without breaking the skin of the man's scalp.

Another characteristic skill of the samurai was *iai*, the ability to unsheathe the sword and deliver a fatal blow in one swift movement.

A young samurai was expected to practice his swordsmanship by executing criminals. He could expect to perform his first execution before he turned sixteen.

Horse riders would spend hours practicing *yabusame*: galloping along the firing ranges, controlling their horses with their knees, while shooting arrows at three small wooden targets, and, in some cases, dogs (a practice called *inuoumono*, which was discouraged by Buddhist priests, who eventually managed to persuade the samurai to use padded arrow tips to prevent injury to the animals).

LIVING QUARTERS

Before the Separation Edicts of Toyotomi Hideyoshi (*see page 35*) the samurai would have divided their time between their military and agricultural duties, living in the *daimyo*'s castle and then returning to their own estates. As the separation between samurai and farmer widened, samurai increasingly lived exclusively in the *daimyo*'s headquarters, which was usually a castle.

Early Japanese castles were basic stockades built on a mountain, but over the centuries they developed into huge fortresses, such as those at Osaka and Himeji. The samurai lived in barracks inside the castle walls. The *daimyo* lived in a one-story mansion (*yashiki*) at the center of the castle, and his most high-ranking retainers, the *karo*, were housed close to him. The samurai were housed further out, and the *ashigaru* lived outside the castle walls, along with the less senior retainers, whose distance from the castle walls was proportionate to their status.

CHAPTER 2: Samurai Daily Life

Samurai houses were wooden with high thatched roofs. Inside the quarters were the wooden corridors and translucent sliding wall panels (*shoji*). The outer walls were made of bamboo and covered with plaster. The floors were raised to keep the rooms dry and airy, except in the kitchen which had an earthen floor. The floors were covered with rectangular straw mats called *tatami*, which are still used today.

Furniture and decoration were minimal, clothes were kept in wooden chests, and the beds were rolled away and kept in a cupboard during the day. Heating came from an open fire in the middle of the room or from a box of warm charcoal.

The main room always contained an alcove called a *tokonoma*, which displayed a single object of extreme beauty, such as a scroll, painting, or piece of pottery. The piece was intended to promote contemplation and it was this room in which the tea ceremony was hosted (*see page 66*).

The toilets were heavily guarded, as that is where the *daimyo* was at his most vulnerable to ambush.

The samurai garden was an important place of rest, and encouraged contemplation and meditation. It was a work of art, full of the harmonious juxtaposition of opposites (light and shade, hard and soft), and with important sculptural qualities of plants, trees, and materials. Asymmetry, simplicity, maturity, subtlety, transcendence, and stillness were its key elements; they combined to create *shibui*, an elegance and hidden beauty with simple restraint.

The samurai garden also used a Zen principle called *kare san-sui*, or "dry landscape," where rocks, gravel, and sand were used to represent the patterned order of the universe. Rhythmic lines were raked in flowing patterns around the large, asymmetrical stones. One samurai had a garden made entirely of sand, which flowed like water.

EATING AND DRINKING

A samurai was expected to eat and drink frugally. One of the samurai chronicles describes a shogun's New Year's banquet consisting of only a bowl of rice and a cup of *sake* ("rice wine").

The daily diet was simple but highly nutritious—based mainly on rice, vegetables, soy bean products, fish, and fruit. However, the most devout Buddhist samurai would not eat any meat.

A *daimyo*'s wealth was measured by how much rice his land could yield (*koku*). One *koku* was the amount of rice that could feed one person for a year. The total number of *koku* a *daimyo*'s land yielded indicated how many soldiers he should muster for his lord if summoned to war. Most samurai ate husked rice, and the daily ration (which was also his wage) for an *ashigaru* ("foot soldier") weighed about two pounds. Richer samurai enjoyed polished rice, which was often sweetened.

During peacetime the samurai enjoyed hunting, and thus were able to supplement their diets with duck, deer, or wild boar. The majority of their everyday animal protein came from eating a wide variety of seafood and shellfish.

Etiquette has always been an important part of Japanese dining. Dining inside the *daimyo*'s *yashiki* would have been accompanied by much ceremony. But even a low ranking samurai would have observed scrupulous dining hygiene and etiquette.

LEISURE PURSUITS

When the samurai weren't fighting they had plenty of time for relaxation (especially when they no longer tended their own fields). They were great patrons of the arts and they enjoyed poetry and calligraphy. Even flower arranging was an important samurai pastime and martial art because it trained the eye, hand, mind, and aesthetic sense.

The samurai also enjoyed playing board games of strategy and tactics such as *go* and *shogi* ("Japanese chess").

Education was vital for a samurai because social networking was an important part of being an effective military leader, and the interaction between samurai further strengthened their already close bonds.

When traveling *biwa* (a "short-necked lute") performers put on a show for the *daimyo*, the theme would often be one of moral instruction, or they would recite epic poetry describing the exploits of great samurai from the past.

The most popular pastime was the tea ceremony which, with its elaborate ritual, exemplified the perfect marriage of aesthetic and social expression. The detailed and intricate patterns of movements which the tea master performed as he prepared the beverage echoed the *kata* that the samurai used to seek perfection in swordsmanship. The tea ceremony was a kind of "inner martial art" that was considered a vital expression of the samurai's aesthetic understanding.

But leisure wasn't all about board games and tea; there were many establishments in the towns that grew up around the castles where a samurai could enjoy a more rambunctious evening of heavy drinking and prostitutes.

BUSHIDO

The code of conduct by which a samurai lived and died was known as *bushido* or "the Way of the Warrior." It developed as an unwritten code during early samurai history. Absolute loyalty to the *daimyo* and bravery to protect him with their own lives were the most important of its principles.

As Hojo Shigetoki, writing in the thirteenth century, points out, the master should be obeyed even when he is in the wrong or unreasonable:

"When one is serving officially or in the master's court, he should not think of a hundred or a thousand people, but should consider only the importance of the master. Nor should he draw the line at his own life or anything else he considers valuable. Even if the master is being phlegmatic . . ." A samurai's reward was the "divine protection of the gods and Buddhas."

The closest contemporary Western version of *bushido* is the idea of chivalry. Both systems look back to the exploits of warriors and ancestors of the past, and create idealistic and sometimes largely fictionalized standards of conduct. But while chivalry includes the idea of courtly love, there is no such element in *bushido*.

The final rationalization of *bushido*, and its greatest tenet, was introduced during the seventeenth century, when a samurai was expected to exemplify the Confucian idea of the "superior man" and set a virtuous example to the lower classes.

During the Tokugawa period, the *Bushido Shoshinshu (Bushido for Beginners)*, written by Taira Shigesuke, served as a comprehensive explication of the rules and expectations of *bushido*. Like the *Hagakure* it also begins with a consideration of death:

"One who is supposed to be a warrior considers it his foremost concern to keep death in mind at all times, every day and every night . . . as long as you keep death in mind at all times, you will also fulfill the ways of loyalty and familial duty."

Awareness of mortality was seen as the spur to good conduct, since complacency bred laziness and inattentiveness. A samurai who trained himself to live as though each day were his last would not engage in futile arguments, indulge in unhealthy desires, neglect his duties, or form an unhealthy attachment to material possessions and comforts.

In addition to death, it was also essential for a samurai to keep the spirit of combat in his mind. Taira Shigesuke advises: "For this reason, really serious warriors even wear an edgeless sword or wooden sword to the bath." Being combat-ready even extended to sleeping. Hojo Nagauji advised his samurai to "be soundly asleep at night before eight o'clock, for thieves are most likely to break in between midnight and two in the morning. Having useless long conversation at night, one will be asleep between twelve and two, his money will be taken, and damage will be done."

In *bushido*, familial duty was a fundamental priority as parents were the most recent link in the chain that connected the samurai to their ancestors. Just as a samurai was expected to obey his master, parents too commanded complete respect. Shiba Yoshimasa, a fourteenth-century warrior, instructed that "even if one's parents are lacking in wisdom, if one will follow their precepts he will first of all likely not be turning his back on the Way of Heaven."

One of the biggest challenges for a *daimyo* was recruiting and retaining an army, and while *bushido* provided social cohesion for his samurai, a *daimyo* didn't rely on it alone when it came to his conscript infrastructure. As samurai scholar F. W. Seal acknowledges, "The idea of military requirement provides one with as complex a subject as any relating to the sixteenth century. This is all the more due to the fact that most *daimyo* had their own ideas on how to assess requirement and thus raise armies." He describes how some offered tax breaks in return for soldiers: "In forming a manpower pool from which to draw on, the Takeda of Kai declared that certain segments of the populace were to be considered *gun'yakusho*, or "military taxpayers." These villages received a tax break in return for providing men for military service. In this case, *gun'yakusho* villages were excused 60 percent of their income, whereas standard cultivators (*so-byakusho*) were excused only 45 percent."

Other more powerful *daimyo* were less flexible. The Hojo family issued comprehensive drafts, such as this one from 1560: "All men from 15 to 70 years of age are ordered to come; not even a monkey tamer will be let off . . . men to be permitted to remain in the village are those whose ages are above 70 years, or under 15 years, and too young to be used as messengers, but the others are all ordered to come." However, when it came to arming the rank and file, the same draft highlights the amateur nature of these conscript armies which were rarely equipped with any uniformity: "Men must arrive at the appointed place properly armed with anything they happen to possess, and those who do not possess a bow, a spear, or any sort of regular weapon are to bring even hoes or sickles."

ANCESTORS

Ancestors, pedigree, and lineage were the basis of a samurai's honor and also played an important part in the ritualization of combat. Early war chronicles preface a fight between two samurai with each warrior's recitation of a list of his ancestors and their exploits. By the fourteenth century, with the lineages growing ever longer, they were written on war banners and taken to the battlefield.

Lineage was a precious gift that the samurai had the responsibility of maintaining through his courageous and honorable actions in battle, as mentioned in the war banner of Asuke Jiro: "My name will be praised throughout the whole world and bequeathed to my descendants as a glorious flower."

A complete record of the family tree was kept safely at home. It was considered so precious that the *Hagakure* describes an incident where a samurai ran into a burning mansion to rescue his lord's family tree document. He didn't come out, but when the fire was put out, the genealogy was found safe: before he succumbed to the smoke the man had cut open his own stomach and tucked the genealogy inside to protect it from the flames.

Through this ancestor veneration, dead warriors symbolically lived on in the deeds of the living warriors who used their conduct as a reference point for their own achievements.

In the sixteenth century, samurai started wearing a small flag called a *sashimono* at the back of the suit of armor to identify themselves and their lineage. By then, battle banners and declarations had become impractical as the style of fighting changed to one where the battle was initiated by *ashigaru* throwing missile weapons, rather than by two rival samurai having a verbal genealogical exchange.

Another way that samurai attracted notice on the battlefield was by wearing extravagantly customized helmets, such as the gold catfish-tail helmet worn by Maeda Toshiie that increased his height by at least two feet. Other popular adornments included buffalo horns, peacock feathers, and theatrical masks. One family of samurai, the Ii family from the Omi Province, were instantly recognizable because they painted the armor of their entire army, samurai as well as foot soldiers, a brilliant red.

RELIGIOUS BELIEF

The samurai operated in a society that embraced five formative traditions: Shinto-ism, Buddhism, Confucianism, Taoism, and folk religion.

It is easy to see how elements from various religions shaped samurai philosophy and practices. For example, samurai mastery over the fear of death comes from Buddhism and the idea of reincarnation, while the earlier Shinto religion, with its focus on ances-tors, provides *bushido* with its strain of loyalty and patriotism; Confucianism provides a framework for moral interactions between master and servant, family and friends. Confucianism valued an ordered society where everyone knew where they fit into the hierarchy. It was also a very practical religion that valued deeds above contemplation and discussion. Leadership was about setting a virtuous example rather than rhetoric. The most important Confucian values were *ko* ("filial piety") and *chu* ("loyalty"), which are central ethical tenets of *bushido*. Swordsmanship was always linked to the samurai's need to protect and serve his master.

The discipline of self-denial comes from Zen Buddhism. The samurai sought to channel body, mind, spirit, and weapon through action towards the attainment of selflessness, enlightenment, and complete emptiness.

This is a very different approach to the way that Western troops are trained to be fearless. In both systems, rituals and routines instill unquestioning obedience, but in the West there is no spiritual dimension and a greater emphasis on desensitiza-tion and erecting mental blocks to fear and the horrors of war, rather than the samurai focus of emptying the mind.

Ritual, religion, and daily life were inseparable, as there were rituals for everything from saying prayers before battle to planting rice in the fields and the elaborate tea ceremony. Samurai did not go to weekly religious services at the temple; instead, they visited when they needed to say a prayer, especially before departing for war when they would pray for victory.

SEPPUKU

The ultimate expression of loyalty to one's master was a samurai's willingness to commit ritual suicide (*seppuku*) if he brought disgrace to him through failure, in sympathy following his lord's death, or to avoid the disgrace of capture after losing a battle. Suicide as a response to personal failure was called *sokotsu-shi*.

Seppuku was usually performed by slicing open the abdomen with a *tanto* ("dagger"), and then enduring a slow and painful death. This belly-cutting method was also called *hara kiri*. Sometimes, another samurai would act as his second, or *kaishakunin*, and behead the dying man to shorten his agony. When cutting the head, the second aimed to leave the head hanging from a small flap of skin, to prevent it from rolling around on the floor in an undignified manner.

It took a loyal friend, indeed, to act as *kaishakunin*, since, as Yamamoto Tsunetomo points out, "From ages past it has been considered ill-omened by samurai to be requested as *kaishakunin*. The reason for this is that one gains no fame even if the job is well done. And if by chance one should blunder, it becomes a lifetime disgrace." That lifetime of disgrace wouldn't last long if a *kaishakunin* chose to commit *sokotsu-shi*.

The earliest written reference to *seppuku* is in the war chronicle *Hogen Monogatari*, recounting a conflict in 1156. It describes the swift capture of samurai Uno Chikaharu and his men, who "had no time to unsheathe their swords or slice their stomachs."

The dignity with which Minamoto Yorisama performed *seppuku* following his defeat at the battle of Uji in 1180 provided an example for subsequent generations of samurai. Before dying he wrote this poem on the back of his *tessen* ("war fan"):

Like an aged tree
Which yields no blossoms
Cheerless my life has been
Destined to bear no fruit.

Since then, there have been numerous other recorded examples of *seppuku*, some of which were extravagant. The veteran warrior Yamamoto Kansuke is famous for committing *seppuku* by running headlong into the enemy after his perceived failure at the fourth battle of Kawanakajima in 1561. He received over eighty wounds before retreating to commit *seppuku*. His noble death was not diminished when his military tactics proved correct, as shortly afterwards reinforcements arrived and his army went on to win the battle.

In contrast, during the Nanbokucho Wars, when Kusunoki Masashige (*see page 184*) failed to hold the mountain castle Akasaka, he built a fire to fool his enemies into thinking he had performed *seppuku*, and escaped to fight another day.

The great samurai general Nitta Yoshisada was defeated in a battle in the Echizen province. Yoshisada's horse was shot and fell, trapping his leg, whereupon he cut off his own head. The *Hagakure* holds him up as an example, not only of a samurai's will, but to suggest that after a warrior's head has been cut off he "should be able to do one more action with certainty. The last moments of Nitta Yoshisada are proof of this. Had his spirit been weak, he would have fallen the moment his head was severed."

Seppuku was expected of anyone found to have had illicit relations with another man's wife, as indicated in the house codes of Chosokabe Motochika: "As to illicit relations with another's wife: Although it is obvious, unless the guilty pair kill themselves, both of them should be executed. If approval of relatives is obtained, revenge may be undertaken, but unnatural cruelty will constitute a crime. If the husband fails to kill the man, or if he is away at the time the offense becomes known, the people of the village should kill the offender."

JUNSHI

Junshi, or "following in death," was *seppuku* performed following the death of the master. The capture of Kamakura in 1333 was followed by a classic act of mass *junshi*, described here in one of the war chronicles:

"The remaining retainers rushed to the middle gate and shouted, 'Our master has taken his life. May all loyal subjects follow his lead!' Then they lit a fire in the mansion, formed a line in the smoke, and slashed their bellies. Not wishing to be bested, three hundred other warriors cut open their stomachs and plunged into the inferno."

However, a samurai wasn't obliged to perform *junshi* after the death of his lord, which is why there were so many masterless *ronin (see page 40)*. Furthermore, this practice did not meet with universal approval, since losing a group of loyal retainers by *junshi* weakened a dynasty even more than the death of its *daimyo* alone.

The first Tokugawa shogun attempted to address this threat to stability by condemning *junshi* in his House Laws of 1616, but two generations later, when his grandson died, five of his retainers committed suicide. The next shogun tried to ban the practice again, saying that the heir would be held responsible and punished if any of his predecessor's retainers killed themselves.

A few years later a retainer of the Okudaira clan committed *junshi*. Although the Okudaira family escaped punishment, the dead man's two sons were made to perform *seppuku* and his two sons-in-law were banished. After that, *junshi* all but died out, although as late as 1912 General Nogi and his wife committed suicide after the death of the Emperor.

HOJO BLOODBATH AT KAMAKURA

The most famous occurrence of mass *seppuku* took place at Kamakura after the Hojo family were defeated during the the Nanbokucho Wars. It is described in great detail in the *Taiheiki* war chronicle, as well as the poems they wrote as they died.

A warrior monk named Fuonji Shinnin wrote this poem on a pillar with his own blood:

Wait for a moment

Crossing together the Shideyama road

Let us speak of the world passing away in time

Another monk wrote a death poem on his own pants then ordered his son to chop his head off; the son obeyed and then stuck his sword through his own belly. Three retainers skewered themselves onto the sword as it stuck out of the son's body.

The closest members of the Hojo family retreated to a cave behind the temple of Toshoji to die. Some of them were worried that the leader Hojo Takatoki wouldn't go through with it, so they killed themselves to set an example. When Hojo Takatoki saw their courage and loyalty, he committed *seppuku* followed by the rest of the clan, a total of 283 men. But the deaths didn't end there. A fire was lit in the hall, and when other warriors saw it, they "sliced their bellies and rushed into the flames, while others inflicted heavy blows on each other with their swords . . . more than eight hundred and seventy men died . . ."

芳年武者无類

相摸守北條髙時

大籏

THE FORTY-SEVEN RONIN OF AKO

There is no better demonstration of the *bushido* ideals of honor and loyalty than the story of the forty-seven *ronin* of Ako, the most celebrated tale in the history of the samurai.

In 1701, the shogun Tokugawa Tsunayoshi wanted to throw a lavish and highly formal New Year's reception for three important imperial envoys. Because the occasion demanded rigorous planning, etiquette, and attention to detail, the shogun appointed Asano Takumi no Kami Naganori from the town of Ako to oversee the intricate formalities. However, Ako was a provincial town, so Lord Asano had to rely on the shogun's Master of Court Etiquette, Kira Kozukeno-suke Yoshinaka, for advice.

Lord Asano sent Kira Yoshinaka several gifts to thank him for his cooperation, but Kira was disappointed by them, and started giving Lord Asano misleading advice that resulted in him making several embarrassing breaches of etiquette. On one occasion Lord Asano turned up at court wearing short pants, as Kira had advised him, only to find that everyone else was wearing long pants.

At the end of the reception, and after enduring these painful humiliations, Lord Asano was on the receiving end of Kira's poor advice once again. Furious with embarrassment, he drew his sword and slashed Kira on the forehead.

It was bad enough that Lord Asano had struck a man in anger, but doing so in the presence of the shogun was a capital offense. The shogun immediately ordered Lord Asano to perform *seppuku*. Lord Asano wrote a farewell poem and committed suicide. His lands were forfeited, and his forty-seven loyal retainers became masterless *ronin*.

The forty-seven *ronin* vowed to avenge their master's death, even though they knew that they, too, would be ordered to commit *seppuku* if successful. Kira,

fearing that his life was in danger, increased his personal guard, making the task of killing him almost impossible.

However, the *ronin* bided their time, and spent the following year pretending to have fallen into a life of dissipation, drinking, and prostitutes, knowing that they were being watched closely by Kira's spies. The leader of the *ronin*, Oishi Kuranosuke, even left his wife to go undercover as a fornicator and drunken brawler. So convincing was his charade that, on one occasion, a samurai from Satsuma spat on him in disgust, saying that he was a disgrace to the samurai class.

Finally, when Kira thought the forty-seven *ronin* were no longer a threat, on December 14, 1702, dressed in armor they had secretly made, they breached his mansion defenses and decapitated him. They took the head to the grave of their Lord Asano, and then turned themselves in.

As expected, the shogun immediately ordered them to perform *seppuku*, which they dutifully carried out. After their death, the samurai from Satsuma, who had spat on Oishi, performed *seppuku* to atone for his insults.

The actions of the forty-seven *ronin* have been much debated ever since. Yamamoto Tsunetomo, author of the *Hagakure*, believed that they should not have taken any action, since the shogun's order to Asano to kill himself should have ended the matter. Others, such as Confucian scholar Sato Naotaka, criticized the *ronin* for taking so long to avenge their master's death, since by doing so they risked Kira dying of natural causes (he was in his sixties). He also criticized them for not performing *seppuku* immediately after killing Kira, rather than throwing themselves on the mercy of the shogun, which made them appear to be holding out for a lesser sentence.

Despite the controversy surrounding their actions, the forty-seven *ronin* have nevertheless become Japanese heroes who hold legendary status for their devotion, and people today still visit Sengakuji temple in Shinagawa where Asano and his loyal *ronin* are buried.

Ashikaga Takauji

1305–1358

Ashikaga Takauji was one of the most controversial of the samurai. In a span of just a few years he managed to bring an end to the Hojo *shikken*, restore the imperial court, and then cause a split in the court that would last thirty-five years beyond his death. Takauji founded the Ashikaga shogunate, one of the three most enduring administrations of Japan's feudal time. Takauji's rule began in 1338, beginning the Muromachi period of Japan. He was a descendant of the Seiwa Genji line of samurai, which had settled in the Ashikaga area of Shimotsuke Province (now the Tochigi Prefecture), and a descendant of Emperor Seiwa. Because Takauji was descended from the emperor, he was one of the few leaders to carry the full title of *Sei-i-tai* shogun.

Prior to his elevation to *Sei-i-tai* shogun, Takauji was a general in the Kamakura shogunate, and was sent in 1333 to Kyoto to help end the two-year-old Genko Rebellion. Takauji was disappointed with the Kamakura shogunate, however, and ultimately betrayed the orders of the Hojo *shikken* and allied himself with the deposed Emperor Go-Daigo, Nitta Yoshisada, and Kusunoki Masashige. The alliance was able to take Kyoto. The events restored the imperial court in Kyoto as the ruling position, rather than the military government of the samurai.

Takauji created an office in Kyoto called the *Buygo-sho*. The *Buygo-sho* ran the city, and Takauji assumed the right to hand out rewards, jobs, and promotions to his troops. Go-Daigo generously rewarded Takauji and named him the

足利尊氏

shugo of Musashi and *Chinjufu* shogun—general of the northern pacification command. Takauji, however, had made it clear he wanted the title of shogun, acknowledging that he was Japan's top soldier. The *Chinjufu* shogun title was Go-Daigo's answer to a predicament; it was a step down from the title to which Takauji believed himself entitled, but avoided angering the emperor's other key general, Nitta Yoshisada.

The re-establishment of imperial court power left the samurai clans discontent and neither Takauji nor the emperor was able to prevent a rebellion—the Nakasendai rebellion began in 1335 to try to re-establish the shogunate at Kamakura. In what turned out to be a poor political decision, Go-Daigo sent Nitta Yoshisada rather than Takauji to reclaim Kamakura.

Takauji took offense and defeated Yoshisada at the Battle of Hakone Take no Shita. The *Sei-i-tai* shogun then led his troops to Kyoto, briefly taking the city before being rebuffed by Yoshisada and Kusunoki Masashige. Takauji retreated to Kyushu, where he recruited more soldiers from the local clans and launched a second assault on the capital. In 1336, Takauji defeated Yoshisada and killed Masashige at the Battle of Minato River, taking Kyoto for good and seeing to the installation of Komyo as emperor. That choice caused a north-south split in the court that was not repaired until Takauji's grandson, Ashikaga Yoshimitsu, reunited the two sides in 1392.

Baba Nobufusa
(Nobuharu)
1514-1575

Baba Nobufusa—later known as Baba Nobuharu—was one of the best of Takeda Shingen's Twenty-Four Generals. Reputed to have engaged in twenty-one battles without receiving a single wound, Nobufusa served under three Takeda generations: Nobutora, Shingen, and Katsuyori. He hailed from the Baba clan of the Kai region.

The son of Baba Torasada, Nobufusa fought at most of Shingen's battles, including the fourth Kawanakajima in 1561, Minowa in 1566, Mimasetoge in 1569, and Mikatagahara in 1573. He served Shingen as a senior retainer and had been given Fukashi Castle in Shinano in 1550. Upon the death of Hara Toratane in 1564, Nobufusa received the title of *Mino no Kami*.

Although he enjoyed a close relationship and high standing with Shingen, Nobufusa did not get along as well with Shingen's son, Katsuyori. Nobufusa's loyalty to the Takeda clan won out, however, and despite his better judgment Nobufusa led his troops against Oda Nobunaga at the Battle of Nagashino in 1575. The battle was horrific, with an estimated 10,000 Takeda troops killed on a single June morning. Nobufusa was not injured; he was able to command his men as they protected Katsuyori's retreat across the Kansagawa River. Once Katsuyori was safe, Nobufusa turned his men against the advancing Oda soldiers and was killed in the ensuing fight.

馬場信春

CHAPTER 3
Samurai Armor and Clothing

The earliest form of Japanese armor, called *tanko* ("short armor"), has been found in ancient Japanese burial mounds from the Kofun period (A.D. 300-700). Designed for infantry fighting (rather than horseback), it was very heavy, only protected the chest and belly, and was difficult to put on. As with all subsequent Japanese armor, the metal components were lacquered to prevent rusting, and to repel arrows and other weapons off their smooth surface.

Plates of iron were fitted close to the body and held together with leather strips (often made from deer hide). At the front was an opening which was tied up with cloth. The wearer had to spring open the whole suit to get it on, but later models had hinges fitted at the side for this purpose. A pair of cloth shoulder straps helped to take most of the armor's weight off the hips and move it to the shoulders.

The shoulders and arms were covered with a series of curved plates, resembling an armadillo's back armor. At the elbow these were replaced by a panel of defensive scales (*kozan*). The neck was covered with U-shaped overlapping strips of iron laced with leather thongs.

The hips, thighs, groin, and backside were protected with a flared skirt of plates called a *kusazuri* (which literally means "grass rubber"), that ended just above the knee. It consisted of several horizontal pieces laced together with leather straps. Baggy pants were worn on the lower legs which were left unprotected.

Although this armor was very functional, it had some decorative features, including leather thongs on the body and pheasant-tail feathers on the *kabuto* ("helmet").

LAMELLAR ARMOR

Lamellar armor, consisting of a number of identical small overlapping plates of metal, is thought to have originated in the Middle East and come to Japan through Korea. The Japanese version, called *keiko*, was developed for mounted warriors, and by the end of the sixth century A.D. it had virtually superseded the *tanko*. Its flexibility made it easy to wear and it absorbed the energy from a blow more effectively.

The basic *keiko* was a sleeveless coat of plates with a front opening and a flared thigh-length skirt. The collar and upper arm guards were also made entirely of scales, and the plate-defense for the forearms was replaced by narrow vertical splints. More plate-work protected the legs, and was tied at the back.

The early helmets had been peaked, and over time this became more prominent, with geometric fretwork and a circular cup around the top. The neck guard was little changed.

KABUTO

The *kabuto* ("helmet") was the most eyecatching piece of a samurai's armor and served the dual function of protection and status symbol. The *Hagakure* advises: "While ornamentation on armor is unnecessary, one should be very careful about the appearance of his helmet. It is something that accompanies his head to the enemy's camp." Very rich samurai wore *kabuto* made from gold-plated copper.

The *kabuto* was made up of several components: *hachi* ("bowl"), *mabisashi* ("peak"), *maedate* ("crest"), *shikoro* ("neck guard"), and *fukigayeshi* ("winglets").

The helmet was constructed of several riveted plates. Early helmets only had a few plates, but by the seventeenth century as many as 120 plates were used in *suji-bachi*-style multi-plate helmets. The rivets were also an important feature. In early helmets they were prominent and decorative, gradually shrinking in size through time, until by the fifteenth century they were filed flat.

At the center of the helmet's crown was a hole called a *tehen*. If the samurai had a long *motodori* ("pigtail"), he would feed it through the *tehen*. Some scholars believe this feature was primarily for ventilation or a result of the riveting process, although it clearly became desirable as some types of three-plated helmet actually had *tehen* deliberately cut out of them.

The *shikoro* ("neck guard") was riveted to the helmet and consisted of three to seven rows of metal plates, held together with silk braids and leather thongs, and reinforced by stiff leather and many smaller plates. The lowest row, called the *hishinui-no-ita*, was often lined with leather to stop it from bashing on the *sode* ("shoulder plates").

The top plates of the neck guard were folded back to form the *fukigayeshi*, which protected against downward cuts aimed at the lacing. The *fukigayeshi* was often decorated with the samurai's *mon* (*see page 167*). They became smaller over time, so that by end of the sixteenth century they were little more than ear-like flanges coming out from the top-most plate. Some later helmets had no *fukigayeshi* at all.

Underneath the helmet, a cap called an *eboshi* and a *hachimaki* ("headband") were usually worn. The *daimyo* and their important retainers wore an *eboshi* made of black silk gauze stiffened with a lacquered paper lining, pinned to the topknot.

After the fourteenth century, a padded inner cap (*uchi-bari*) with straps was incorporated into the helmet to keep the metal away from the skull.

Crests were attached to a socket on the peak called a *haraidate*, and also on the sides of the helmet. Popular choices of crest were twin-horns (*kuwagata*), triple-bladed designs (*mittsu-kuwagata*), antlers, buffalo horns, and crescent moons.

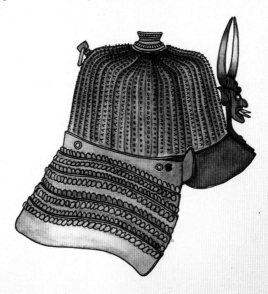

Kabuto Styles

Each helmet was unique and many were designed for a specific individual, but there are a few common styles, including:

hoshi kabuto: overlapping plates are riveted to form a bowl. The helmet is strong and heavy and often has a russet iron finish.

suji kabuto: ribs stand up at the edge of each plate and the *hoshi* are filed away to reduce the weight.

koboshi kabuto: has lots of small, stud-like rivets on the helmet bowl (*koboshi* means "small star").

hari bachi: multi-plate helmet with no ribs, and with the rivets filed flush (*hari* means "spread on").

zunari kabuto: often called the "three-plated helmet." Although *zunari* means "head-shaped," these helmets have a wide range of shapes from pointed to tall domed bowls.

kawari kabuto: these wildly unconventional helmets started to appear after 1600. They are built up with *papier-mâché*, wood, and lacquer to make unusual objects including sea monsters, animal heads, and sea shells.

tatami kabuto: these light-weight and utilitarian folding helmets were popular with the *ashigaru*, as they were easy to take on travels, especially during the time of the alternate attendance system (*see page 38*).

THE O-YOROI

While foot soldiers retained the *keiko* style, by the twelfth century the mounted samurai were wearing the classic samurai armor called the *o-yoroi*, or "great armor," with its characteristic box-shape. It first appeared in the tenth century, during the middle- and late-Heian period.

It was also lamellar, with a combination or iron and leather scales, and while it was relatively light (at about sixty-five pounds) it restricted the samurai's movements when he was dismounted.

The body of the armor, the *do*, consisted of four lamellar boards laced together with silk and leather chords. Attached to each board was the *kusazuri* which protected the lower body. The front of the torso plate was covered by a leather panel called a *tsurubashiri*, which prevented the bowstring from snagging on the scales. This was often decorated ornately with various designs, including Shinto and Buddhist gods.

Two *sode* ("shoulder plates") were attached to the *do* with *watagami* ("shoulder straps") and tied together at the back with a decorative tassel called an *agemaki*. The *sode* were *o-sode*, *chu-sode*, or *ko-sode* ("large," "medium," or "small").

Two asymmetrical plates, called the *sendan no ita* and *kyubi no ita*, protected the underarm area. Later, *wakabiki* armpit protectors were worn, with varieties distinguished by the method of fastening, such as *botangake* ("with buttons"), *kohaze-gake* ("with hooks"), and *himo-tsuki* ("with cords").

The *o-yoroi* was popular among the samurai until the fourteenth century, when fighting on foot increased, and they further developed the lighter *do-maru* armor worn by the *ashigaru*, which was more rounded, with smaller shoulder guards.

The style of *odoshi* ("lacing") varied over time too. The lacing of the individual plates is called *shitagarami*, whereas *odoshi* refers to the suspensory and decorative lacing. The origin of the word is thought to come from *odosu*, which means "to scare," hence the bright colors used for the *odoshige* ("lacing hair").

Kebiki odoshi ("closed space or full lacing") was the oldest style, a thick lacing with no gaps. This expensive and labor-intensive lacing method gave way to the cheaper and simpler method of *sugake odoshi* ("sparce-point lacing"), in which pairs of braids were used, topped with an X. *Hishiniu*, an even easier method using cross-knots, was used on breastplates.

The colors and patterns of lacing were used to identify individual samurai clans. For example, the Taira clan used purple, the Fujiwara light green, and the Tachibana yellow. The different colored cords had their own names as well: light blue was called *hanairo-odoshi*, and navy blue *kon-odoshi*. Lacing of many colors was called *iroiro-odoshi*. If a samurai did not expect to survive his next battle, he might use lacing of white, the Japanese color of mourning.

By the sixteenth century the armor became known as *tosei gusoku* ("modern armor"). It included face masks, *suneate* (shin guards made of vertical plates connected by hinges and sometimes lined with material, with a leather guard attached to the inner side to prevent the stirrup from rubbing when riding), *haidate* (thigh guards—apron-like pieces of cloth fringed with overlapping plates of metal), and flags called *sashimono* (*see page 169*).

There are many variations on the *do* ("body armor"), the most common of which were the *niuinobe do* and the *mogami do*. Lacquering was taken to the extreme in the *yukinoshita do*, where the many layers created a very smooth surface to deflect arrowheads, sword blades, and arquebus balls.

1.   2.   3.

The okegawa do is put on in six stages, as follows:

1. Sit in the position illustrated.

2. Take the *do* towards you and open the *hikiawase* (the part where the *do* is made to open at the side).

3. Take the *hikiawase* in your right hand and put the *do* upon your knee.

The throat was protected by a *nodowa* which was fastened at the back of the neck with cords. Variations on the *nodowa* are the *meguriwa*, which is attached with hooks; the *eriwa*, which is attached with a buckle; and the *manjuwa,* which is fastened to the lower part of the mask and the upper part of the breastplate.

4. **5.** **6.**

4. Put your left hand and arm into the *do* and pull it until it entirely covers your body.

5. Fold the front part of the *hikiawase* on to the back part, and then tie the cords attached to the upper part firmly in the knot called *hanamusubi* ("flower-shaped knot").

6. Fasten the cords which are generally called *kurisage no o*, beginning on the left side of your waist; pull one towards the back and the other towards the front, passing the back cord through the ring which is attached to the right side of the body, and tying the ends in front. These cords will be best made of twisted cotton cloth, cut into halves from ordinary width. Silk cords are made, but are not good for actual use.

Tanki Yoriaku by Hayakawa Kyuukei, 1735, translation by Matt Garbutt, 1911

FACE MASK

There are six basic styles of mask, some with a movable nose-piece. Most had moustaches so that decapitated heads would not be mistaken for those of women and discarded. Before the mask was put on, a handkerchief called a *fukusa* was placed between the mask and chin.

The *mempo* ("face cheek") mask covered the whole face; the *hoate* ("cheek protector") covered the face from below eye level; the *sarubo* ("monkey cheek") only covered the cheeks and chin; and the *tsubamegata* ("swallow pattern") only protected the chin. The most popular was the *hoate*.

The style of mask changed over the centuries. In the twelfth century the *happuri* only covered the temples and the forehead, but later masks covered the whole face, and even later the style reverted to a half-mask.

The inside of the mask was lacquered (often red) for comfort, and the shape was designed to follow the contours of the face. At the bottom of the mask was a small hole, often with a tiny pipe attached, to allow perspiration to drip out.

With the introduction of the face mask, it was possible to send onto the battle-field a decoy *daimyo* called a *kagemusha* (literally "shadow warrior"), made more convincing if he was carrying the *daimyo*'s personal standard. However, there is no mention of this practice in any of the war chronicles.

SAMURAI CLOTHING

When wearing armor, the samurai would wear a *fundoshi* ("loincloth") made of hemmed white linen or cotton, about five feet in length. A cord at the top was worn in a loop over the neck, and bottom cords were tied around the waist. The *Hagakure* recommends the wearing of badger skin underwear on campaign, to prevent lice. Over this was worn a *kimono*, a long wide-sleeved silk garment, cinched at the waist by a sash-like *obi* ("belt"), which was wrapped two or three times around the body and tied at the front. A typical *obi* was six to nine feet long. On top of this high-ranking samurai wore a two-piece *yoroi-hitatare* ("armor robe"), with jacket and pants tucked into *kiahan* ("gaiters"). The *kiahan* were made of linen or cotton cloth tied at the inside of the leg.

When not wearing armor, the *kimono* was the standard attire. A light silk one was worn during the summer, and a thicker one during the winter. The *katana* and *wakizashi* were tucked into the *obi*. In colder weather a pair of loose samurai pants, called *hakama*, was worn over the *kimono*. These were either split between the legs like pants or non-split, like a skirt, with a low crotch and large openings at the side, tied at the front and rear. In a combat emergency, the *hakama* could be quickly tucked into the belt to keep it away from the legs.

In the Edo period, very-high ranking samurai wore pants called *nagabakama* on formal occasions. The legs of these pants were so long that they covered the feet and trailed behind the wearer as he walked. They were very difficult to walk in, and so it was considered the height of good taste and breeding to wear them without tripping over them. It was also a useful way of ensuring that the wearer could not cause trouble at court.

Footwear consisted of socks called *tabi*, with a separate space for the big toe. There were two main types of socks: *kawa-tabi* ("tanned skin socks," often printed with patterns) and *momen-tabi* ("cotton cloth socks"). There were also *momi-tabi* ("red silk socks"), but according to *Tanki Yoriaku*, an arming guide written by Hayakawa Kyuukei in 1735, "they are only used by very effeminate persons."

Straw sandals called *waraji* were made out of various materials, including hemp, myouga stalks (a kind of ginger), palm fibers, cotton thread, and rice straw. The sandals were tied securely to the feet using a variety of methods, including *nakachi-nuki, yotsu-chigake, takano-gakevario. Tanki Yoriaku* recommends:

"It is very important to use a **nakagukuri** *or extra tie across the instep, as this will be a great help in marching on steep, snowy, or muddy roads, and in crossing swamps or rivers, in any case you must not forget the* **nakagukuri** *when marching on hard roads."*

Wooden clogs, called *geta*, were sometimes worn in times of leisure, but never in combat.

Yugake ("gloves") were made of tanned skin, and sometimes had a small hole in the palm called an *inome*.

When it rained, a straw raincoat called a *kappa* was worn, and an ornate folding umbrella was carried. A large straw hat, called a *kasa*, shielded against both the sun and rain.

By the Edo period the *hitatare* was largely replaced by the *kamishimo*, a two-piece costume worn over the *kimono*. The upper garment, the *kataginu*, was a sleeveless jacket with large shoulders, and the lower part was still the *hakama*. Both parts were of the same color and pattern and had the *daimyo's mon* on the chest and the back. The *kamishimo* was usually worn outside the house or when visitors were expected, while the *kimono* was acceptable for everyday indoor wear.

Bright outlandish colors were considered undignified and conceited, so muted tones were the norm, although children were dressed much more extravagantly until their *genpuku* ("coming-of-age") ceremony, when adult muted colors were adopted.

SAMURAI HAIR

A samurai's hairstyle was a vital part of his appearance. If even so much as a hair was out of place, this was considered disgraceful, so the hair was oiled to keep it in one mass.

The ubiquitous *chomage* ("topknot") was a customary way of tying up the obligatory *motodori* ("pigtail"). The origin of the pigtail is inconclusive, though it probably started in ancient China and was brought to Japan between the Asuka-Nara and Heian periods.

The pigtail was either made by the *chasen gami* method, where string was wound round the lower half of the pigtail to make it stick out at the end, like a tea whisk; or the *mitsu-ori* method which was popular in the late sixteenth century, involved forming the hair into a cylinder then bending it forward, back, and forward again before tying it in place. A variation on this style was the *futatsu-ori*, in which the cylinder was only folded forward, and then the front was trimmed with a razor.

In illustrations of combat, defeated samurai are often depicted with messy hair. From the early sixteenth century the hair was shaved off at the front (this was called the *sakayaki*), to make wearing a helmet more comfortable. This fashion was copied by lower ranks of Japanese society. Instead of trimming the forelock, young samurai formed it into a triangle. Samurai who were also Buddhist monks often shaved their heads completely.

ACCESSORIES

A samurai carried several accessories with him on campaign, including:

kate-bukuro: a provision bag carried at the side of the waist, commonly made of twisted paper strings resembling fine basketwork, and measuring about one foot by nine-and-a-half inches.

kubibukuro: a head bag for carrying the severed head of an enemy, slung from the waist or fastened to a saddle.

saihai: a baton used by high ranking samurai to direct troops.

tenugui: a white cotton cloth towel about three feet long, attached to a ring on the *do*.

uchi-bukuro: a money purse tied around the waist or around the neck; another method of carrying money was to paste coins on a folded strip of thick paper hidden in the underwear.

uchi-gaye: a rice bag which could carry about three or four *gou* (about one pound) of raw rice.

udenuki: a round cord threaded through two holes in the sword's *tsuba* ("hand guard") or *tsuka-gashira* (the head of the sword-hilt) and worn around the wrist to prevent the sword from falling to the ground when dropped.

waraji: a spare pair of sandals carried on campaign.

yo-bukuro: another small pocket tied inside the *sode*, or inside the *kusazuri*, for storing small items such as a handkerchief.

Hattori Hanzo
(Hattori Masanari)
1541-1596

Hattori Hanzo, also known as Hattori Masashige, fought in his first battle when he was just sixteen years old. Like his father, Hattori Yasunaga, Hanzo served the Tokugawa clan. In a case very much "like father, like son," Yasunaga worked under Matsudaira Hirotada of Mikawa Province; Hanzo served Hirotada's son, the infamous shogun Tokugawa Ieyasu.

He and others were directed to assist Ieyasu's son, Tokugawa Nobuyasu, to commit suicide on Oda Nobunaga's order in 1579. Hanzo, who held Nobuyasu in high regard, could not bring himself to follow the order.

Hanzo fought at Anegawa in 1570 and at Mikatagahara in 1572, but his best-known contribution to the Tokugawa shogunate was his ability to call upon old contacts to help save Ieyasu. The incident occurred in 1582 after Oda Nobunaga's assassination. Ieyasu, along with Hanzo and his other retainers, were staying near Osaka when they learned of Nobunaga's death. They left just in time to avoid capture by Akechi Mitsuhide's soldiers, but the troops pursued them.

服部半蔵

Hanzo suggested a route to Mikawa through the Iga province. Hanzo had ties with samurai there and it was an area loyal to Ieyasu, who had protected survivors of Nobunaga's 1580 invasion. Hanzo went ahead to make arrangements and, as he had anticipated, the Iga samurai cooperated. They not only led Ieyasu and his men through the Iga back roads, they also provided an escort to see them safely through the province.

Hanzo, remembered as a ninja leader, was given the rank of *Yoriki* after the Tokugawa shogunate move to Kanto in 1590. With the title came the command of 200 troops that would become the Edo Castle guard under Hanzo's son.

Hojo Soun
(Ise Shinkuro, Ise Shozui, Ise Nagauji)

1432-1519

Hojo Soun, ironically, was never known in his lifetime by that name. It was a moniker bestowed four or five years posthumously by Ujitsuna. The samurai was known first as Ise Shinkuro, then Ise Shozui, and later as Ise Nagauji.

As did many others, Nagauji fled Kyoto during the Onin War and went to Suruga with a half-dozen followers. There, he became a retainer of his brother-in-law, Imagawa Yoshitada. When Yoshitada was killed in battle in 1476, Nagauji successfully solved a dispute over succession rights between Yoshitada's cousin, Oshika Norimitsu, and Yoshitada's six-year-old son, Ujichika. The young boy was the rightful successor, but Norimitsu again tried to seize control in 1487. Nagauji killed Norimitsu and was rewarded with a gift of Kokokuji Castle and expanded power and influence.

By 1493, Izu Province was at the early stages of a civil war. Ashikaga Yoshizumi took Kyoto in a coup, becoming the eleventh Ashikaga Shogun, while across the border at Kokokuji Castle, Ise Nagauji saw an opportunity and successfully invaded Izu. He increased the size of his band with former Ashikaga retainers.

北条早雲

The following year the deaths of Ogigayatsu-Uesugi Sadamasa, and the lord of Odawara Castle, Omori Ujiyori, gave Nagauji an opportunity in Sagami. His son, Omori Fujiyori, who had lost both his father and his powerful overlord, succeeded Omori Ujiyori. Nagauji acted as a friend and father figure, working his way into Fujiyori's confidence with gifts and flattery. But in 1495, Nagauji used a deer hunt as a ruse to penetrate Omori territory with his soldiers, surprising a stunned Fujiyori and easily capturing the castle.

Nagauji attacked the Miura clan in 1512. He brought down Okazaki Castle, forcing Miura Yoshiatsu to Arai Castle, but it was another four years before Nagauji and his followers brought down Arai Castle, leading Miura Yoshiatsu and Miura Yoshimoto to commit suicide.

The year Nagauji conquered Izu marked the start of the Sengoku period. Nagauji became known as one of the first examples of *gekokujo*—the weak overcoming the strong—in action, because a little-known samurai had been able to take a province for his own without an imperial decree or the shogun's permission.

CHAPTER 4

Samurai Weaponry

The image of the samurai warrior wielding his sword with both hands is ubiquitous in the public mind. It is hard to dissociate the idea of the sword as weapon from the warrior. However, while there is no dispute that the samurai developed sword technique and manufacturing into an art form, most people are unaware of the vast array of weaponry that was at his disposal. As samurai scholar Stephen Turnbull notes, "the use of the sword is but one stage in a process that begins with the bow, moves through the sword to the dagger, and often ends with bare hands."

YUMI

For many centuries the *yumi*, or longbow, was the primary samurai weapon. The earliest samurai fought on horseback and their exploits were often described in ancient Japanese war stories as *kyba no michi*, or the "Way of the Bow and Horse." The legendary first emperor of Japan, Emperor Jimmu, was always depicted carrying a bow.

A samurai could fire a volley of arrows with incredible speed and accuracy, even at a distance of 150 feet. The arrows could travel twice as far if accuracy were not an issue (e.g. when firing into a crowd of soldiers). Archers would often hide in a high position before a battle, behind a large mobile bamboo shield called a *tedate*. A battle began with a hail of arrows, and the samurai would take advantage of their superior position to cut through the enemy lines.

The samurai used many different types of arrow, each with a specific use. The most innovative samurai arrow had a barbed tip, which inflicted more damage than conventional arrows both on entry and when removed; the barb also gave the arrows greater accuracy and helped them travel longer distances. Samurai also used poison or fire on the tips of their arrows. Some arrows were used purely for signaling. Traditionally, battles began with the firing of a signal arrow. These arrows had bulbous perforated heads which made a whistling sound as they traveled, to alert the *kami* (Shinto gods of Japan) to witness the warriors' brave exploits.

The bow and arrow were the most effective weapons to defend castles from a distance until the introduction of the rifle to Japan in the sixteenth century. They were ineffective as close-range weapons when fighting moved from horse to ground, so they were replaced by swords and spears. The Mongols forced a change of samurai tactics, since they were prepared to shoot horses from beneath riders to force the samurai into ground combat.

A typical samurai bow was about eight feet long; it was made of deciduous wood backed with bamboo and the string was made of hemp coated with wax or pine resin to form a hard, smooth surface. The arrows were made of bamboo, with three feathers attached to the back to form a flight.

The traditional method of firing from a horse involved holding the bow above the head, then moving the hands apart so that when the arrow was released the left arm was straight and the right arm was near the right ear.

By the Sengoku period, bows were rarely fired from horseback. When firing on foot, the samurai developed a technique of holding the bow horizontally and level with the waist.

There are numerous accounts which celebrate samurai archery skill. Minamoto Tameto sank an enemy ship by piercing it with a single arrow struck below the water line. At the battle of Yashima in 1184, the enemy hung a fan from the ship's mast and challenged the samurai to hit it, hoping they would waste their arrows. Despite being on horseback in the water, Nasu no Yoichi hit the moving target on his first attempt.

The longbow was a difficult weapon to master, as it required great strength to draw, and took years of practice for a samurai to master. Samurai practiced their skills by firing at small wooden targets while galloping along at right angles to the target; this became the traditional Shinto martial art of *yabusame*, which is still performed today.

CHAPTER 4: Samurai Weaponry

CROSSBOW

During the sixteenth century, the crossbow was the exclusive weapon of the archery squads of *ashigaru*, but it had been common on the battlefield before then, both in the hand-held form and in the larger siege crossbow which fired stones.

The hand crossbow was a powerful and compact weapon, but its rate of fire was slower than the longbow. It first appeared in Japan in the seventh century and it quickly became an infantry weapon. However, as the use of conscripts declined, so did the infantry's use of the crossbow.

According to Japanese records, the siege crossbow (*oyumi*) was different from Chinese models, some of which were enormous and could fire several bolts simultaneously. In the ninth century a Japanese artisan named Shimaki no Fubito claimed that he had improved on the Chinese version, and that his crossbow rotated so that it could fire stones or arrows in four directions. Use of the *oyumi* died out around the beginning of the twelfth century.

TREBUCHET

The counterweight trebuchet is a familiar weapon in European military history, but the Japanese employed a much less efficient traction trebuchet which used manpower (a team of forty men pulling on ropes) to create the throwing force. It threw stones and bombs known as "Chinese plums" that exploded in mid-air, causing a shower of debris. The Japanese were still using the traction trebuchet years after it had been discarded by China and the West.

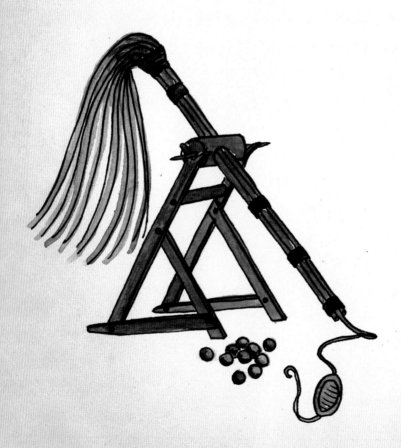

HOKO

Spears were an important part of the samurai's arsenal; symbolically they were important since Japanese myth attributed the formation of the Japanese archipelago to drops of water that fell from the spear of the god Izanagi as he drew it out of the ocean.

The *hoko* was the basic samurai spear. It had four prongs, which made it heavy and unwieldy, so it was later replaced by the straight *yari* (*see page 124*) and the curved *naginata* (*see page 126*).

YARI

The *yari* was a straight-headed polearm that measured anywhere from three to twenty feet. The blade alone could be up to three feet long and had a scabbard (*saya*).

The longest weapons, known as *omi no yari*, were carried by common foot soldiers (*ashigaru*), while the shorter ones, called *mochi yari*, were more popular with the samurai.

An example of a *mochi yari* is preserved today in Tokyo. It was presented to Hattori Hanzo (*see page 112*) by Tokugawa Ieyasu. Its shaft is ten feet long and the blade, which is now broken, would have been four feet long.

The *yari* could be used as a lance while a rider sat in the saddle, or as a slashing weapon while standing in the stirrups.

The tang of the blade was much longer than the sharpened part of the blade and went deep into a hollow part of the shaft (*ebu*), making it very stiff and almost impossible to break off.

The shaft was made of hardwood, such as oak, and then covered in lacquered strips of bamboo held in place by wire or metal rings and attached to a metal pommel (*ishizuki*). The handle would be highly decorated with inlaid metal or flakes of mother-of-pearl.

There were many variations on the basic *yari*, including:

sankuku yari: the tip had a triangular cross-section and no cutting edge, so it was ideal for piercing armor.

kuda yari: the grip had a hollow metal tube which allowed the spear to be spun as it was thrown.

fukuro yari: instead of having the traditional long tang which fit inside the hollow shaft, the blade had a socket on its end that fit over the shaft.

jumonji yari: the blade had two crossbars of equal length sticking out from its base, which curved forward.

katakama yari: the blade had a single crossbar sticking out from the base of the blade, or two crossbars of unequal length.

kikuchi yari: this rare variation is named for the fourteenth-century Kikuchi family of Higo. It looks like a *tanto* (*see page 142*) on a pole.

NAGINATA

This spear consisted of a wooden shaft with a stout single-edged blade at the end that was slightly curved. It also had a sword-like guard (*tsuba*) between the blade and the shaft.

The shaft was usually made to be the height of the bearer's body, and the blade two- to three-feet long. Unlike many other polearms, the shaft was oval in cross-section. At the opposite end was a metal pommel (*ishizuki*) which acted as a counterweight to the blade and enabled the bearer to use both ends in combat. There are several accounts of samurai swinging the *naginata* "like a water wheel." Reizei Motomitsu is described as using this lethal fighting technique during the siege of Ulsan, "slaying 15 or 16 of the nearby enemy before being cut down himself."

The *naginata* was used by *sohei* ("warrior monks") during the eighth century, but its first recorded use in combat was in 1086 in the book *Oshi Gosannenki (A Diary of Three Years in Oshu)*. It really came into its own in the twelfth century when it proved so effective for attacking horse riders that it forced the introduction of *suneate* ("shin guards") to the samurai armor. It later became associated with women, and modern *naginata-jutsu* is studied by more women than men.

With the widespread use of firearms in the seventeenth century, the *naginata* fell into decline, but it still retained its symbolic significance and was often a traditional part of a samurai daughter's dowry. Women were expected to defend their homes while their husbands were away fighting, and the *naginata* was considered the most suitable female weapon for this purpose, since it kept the male opponent at a distance, and relied less upon upper-body strength than the *katana*.

HACHIWARA

The name of this rare sword means "helmet breaker." It had a curved blade with a hook near the handle for catching or breaking the opponent's blade. A *hachi-wara* would have been held in the left hand, while the samurai held a sword in his right. The blades were typically between twelve- and fifteen-inches long. The weapon would not have used thrusting force to split a helmet. Rather, it is likely that the *hachiwara* hooked the helmet and was twisted to crack it open at its riveted joints.

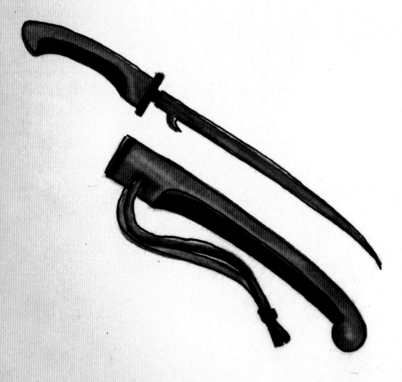

JUTTE

This long iron truncheon was used by the samurai officers in the police force, who were known as *doshin*, as well as by non-samurai police. It was similar to a *hachiwara*, and its function was also to disarm, but the *jutte* was only used as a civil weapon, not in battle. The majority of *jutte* were made of iron, but some were elegantly decorated and gilded with silver (earning them the nickname "silver stick"). Some were made of wood with a metal hook.

KATANA

A type of curved long single-edged sword in use after the 1400s, *katana* is often misused as a blanket term referring to any long Japanese sword. However, a sword is only a *katana* when it is worn with the blade facing upwards through a belt-sash called an *obi*. If attached to the belt by cords, it is called *tachi* (*see page 140*).

The *katana* was the ultimate samurai status symbol. A good sword was expensive to manufacture and was also a work of art, often handed down through many generations of a samurai's family. The samurai developed a strict code of conduct for the use of the sword, called *bushido* (*see page 68*). ·

Japanese mythology says that the first sword was created by the god Izanagi who used it to kill his son, the Fire God. The sword was eventually given to his great grandson, Ninigi-no Mikoto, to reign on Earth, thus making it the first sword to appear in Japan.

When a *katana* was paired with the *wakizashi* (*see page 138*), the two weapons together were called the *daisho*. The *katana* was used for open combat, while the shorter-bladed *wakizashi* was used as a stabbing sidearm, for close combat. In combat the *katana* is mainly used for cutting, but it can also be used for thrusting. It was usually used with a two-handed grip, but there are surviving historical Japanese sword arts that include one-handed techniques as well.

The manufacture of the sword was complex and labor-intensive, involving specialized craftsmen for every part, not least the forging of the blade, which typically took many days and was a sacred art. Typically, one smith would forge the rough shape, a second smith would fold the metal, and specialist polishers, blade sharpeners, and carvers would finish the blade. Often, the sheath, hilt, and *tsuba* ("hand guard") required specialists, too.

Swordsmithing was an honored and highly-respected profession. The swordsmith would be a very dedicated and religious man who took great pride in his work, since forging was as much a spiritual act as one of skill. He usually engraved his name and titles on every sword that he made. Many swordsmiths are as legendary as the samurai themselves.

The most important part of the manufacturing process was the folding of the steel. Steel was repeatedly "folded"—bent over itself and hammered flat to burn off impurities and homogenize the blade, giving the swords their characteristic grain. The finished blade would contain thousands of paper-thin layers.

Masamune (1288-1328) is probably the best known Japanese swordsmith, as well as a well-known philosopher. He worked in the Sagami Province during the last part of the Kamakura Era and created the *Soshu* tradition of sword-making that was handed down to his ten disciples. He used four bars of welded steel, doubled five times to make 2,097,152 laminations of metal. His blades were so distinctive he did not need to sign them.

The antithesis to the deeply spiritual Masamune was an "evil" swordsmith called Muramasa, whose swords were supposed to bring misfortune to their owners. Unable to stop killing, the owners eventually turned the swords on themselves.

The skill of the forger also lay in creating the perfect blend of hard and soft metal: hard for a strong cutting edge and outer zone (*uagane*); soft in the iron core (*shingane*), which gave springy resilience.

After the blade had reached its final shape, it underwent a process called selective quench hardening. The blade was coated in a stiff paste of clay and water, then a small amount of clay was carefully removed from the cutting edge and the blade was heated to hardening temperature and quickly immersed in cold water. In this way, only the cutting edge would be hardened, and the clay-coated portion of the covered blade would not.

Finally, the long process of polishing began, first with a coarse abrasive stone, then with a succession of finer-grained stone. After polishing, the blade would display the characteristic wavy line known as the *yakiba*, the boundary between the hardened and unhardened metal. The hardened cutting edge could then be sharpened to create the sharpest blade anywhere in the contemporary world.

According to Japanese legend a superior sword was supposed to be strong enough to cut through a stack of seven corpses and sharp enough that when placed in a flowing stream it would cut through a water lily that happened to float past.

The curvature of the blade also played a major part in its legendary power. It allowed the hard and soft parts of the cutting edge to slice into an opponent along a small area, which would then open up as the blade continued to travel. The fact that the samurai never used shields meant that they could wield their swords with two hands for greater speed and force. The *katana* was both sword and shield; by contrast, the technique of blocking and parrying with swords didn't evolve in Europe until the late sixteenth century. Furthermore, the *katana* was the only sword of its time capable of parrying without breaking. Each part of the weapon has a specific name. The scabbard is called a *saya*, and the hand guard the *tsuba*. Every aspect of the weapon was constructed with painstaking artistry.

Each blade has a unique profile, depending on the smith, the construction method, and a bit of luck. The most prominent is the middle ridge, or *shinogi*. The *shinogi* could be placed near the back of the blade for a longer, sharper, more fragile tip, or near the center of the blade for a more moderate *shinogi*. The sword also has an exact tip shape, which is considered an extremely important characteristic: the tip can be long (*o-kissaki*), medium (*chu-kissaki*), short (*ko-kissaki*), or even hooked backwards (*ikuri-o-kissaki*).

Almost all blades are decorated with designs and grooves cut into them. File markings are cut into the hilt-section of the blade (the tang), which was never cleaned, because it was designed to show how the blade steel ages. The practical use of the grooves was to create an uneven surface which bites well into the hilt.

The diagram below shows a selection of tang grooves and their names:

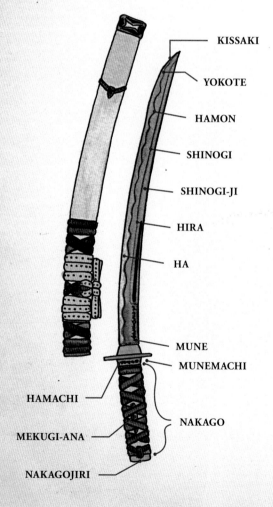

KISSAKI

YOKOTE

HAMON

SHINOGI

SHINOGI-JI

HIRA

HA

MUNE

MUNEMACHI

HAMACHI

NAKAGO

MEKUGI-ANA

NAKAGOJIRI

THE CHANGING SHAPE OF THE JAPANESE SWORD

The Japanese sword blade has changed shape many times over the course of samurai history, as a response to the change of battle tactics and armor.

The earliest blades, made before A.D. 900, were straight and flat with either a chisel-type edge and chisel-shaped points (*kamasu kissaki*); or curved and sometimes double-edged (*kissaki*). These blades were probably heavily influenced by contemporary Chinese blades.

Kissaki moroha-zukuri blades were in use around the same time. They had a curved *shinogi-zukuri* blade with the sharpened kissaki extending up to half the length of the non-cutting side (*mune*). The most famous example of this type of blade is the *Kogarasu-Maru Tachi* made circa A.D. 900.

Early single-edged *shinogi-zukuri* blades were long and narrow cavalry sabers with most of the curvature near the bottom. Over time they became more substantive and wider.

The common shape of Japanese swords first appeared during the mid-Kamakura period. These blades were shorter with less taper.

During the Nanbokucho Wars, blades became wider with large points, but it was the change from cavalry to infantry tactics during the early Muromachi period which saw the most significant change: the birth of the *katana*. The early *katana* was a shortened *tachi*, making it easier to draw while on foot.

During the stable and relatively peaceful Edo period, the classic Shinto sword style emerged: *katana*-length blades that were stout and only slightly curved. By the end of the Edo period, sword-making was in decline, and so many were more decorative than utilitarian, with flamboyant *hamon* (the line between hard and soft metal) and sophisticated *horimono* ("carving").

This period of decadence was followed by a trend that saw a return to the traditional blade styles of the Koto period.

By the time of the Meiji Restoration, traditional Japanese sword-making had all but died out. Since the samurai class was abolished and the wearing of swords was banned, any swords made after 1876 cannot properly be called samurai swords.

WAKIZASHI

This sword has a blade that is, on average, about twenty-inches long; it is similar to the *katana* (*see page 130*), but it is much shorter and thinner, and is used as a close-combat stabbing "sidearm." It came into use during the sixteenth century, gradually replacing the *tanto* ("dagger"—*see page 142*) that had been used in earlier times (except for when a samurai was in armor, when a *tanto* would still be used).

When it is paired with the *katana*, the combination is called the *daisho*. Both swords would have had matching scabbards and fittings.

The *wakizashi* isn't simply a shorter form of *katana*. It was often forged differently and had a different cross-section. The blade is less convex than a *katana* and can therefore slash and cut flesh more aggressively than a *katana*.

Whereas a *katana* would be removed as a sign of peace when the samurai entered a building, the *wakizashi* would be worn at all times. In any case, the *katana* was too long to be used effectively indoors, with the ceilings of feudal Japanese dwellings being low, but the shorter *wakizashi* was ideal. It literally would never leave a samurai's side, from the moment he woke up to when he went to bed and placed it underneath his pillow.

The *wakizashi* served another important function: it was used to perform *seppuku* ("ritual suicide"—*see page 76*).

Since all swords were made for a specific person, the length of the blade depended upon the height of the individual. A *wakizashi* made for a tall man was called an *o-wakizashi*, while one made for a shorter man was called a *ko-wakizashi*.

NODACHI

This is the name given to a field sword with a very long blade first used by samurai in the fourteenth century. Many of these swords were also created as offerings for shrines and temples. They were generally used by samurai on foot, rather than on horseback, and they were effective weapons for breaking the legs of charging cavalry. However, there is a written account of Makara Jurozaemon wielding one from his horse, a feat which would have required considerable physical strength.

The cutting edge was not sharpened all the way to the hilt, and the handle was left round and blunt in a style known as *hamaguri ha* ("clam-shell blade").

TACHI

Slung from the belt with the cutting edge downward, the *tachi* was the classic curved samurai sword which predated the *katana*. Like the *katana*, it required both hands to draw and to use.

It was, on average, about two inches longer than the *katana* and more curved; today these swords are rare because many of them were cut down to form *katana*.

The *tachi* was primarily used by samurai on horseback, where its length was less of a hindrance when it was being drawn. On the ground its length made it unwieldy, which is why it was replaced by the shorter *katana*.

TANTO

The *tanto* is a dagger with a blade length of six to twelve inches, usually with a single cutting edge (but sometimes two). It was used primarily as a stabbing weapon, but it could also slash. The samurai always carried it in his *obi* ("belt"). Before the *wakizashi* became popular, it was also used to perform *seppuku*. It could also be used as a throwing weapon; the martial art of the dagger is called *tanto-jutsu*.

These swords were generally forged without a ridge-line. There are many different styles of *tanto*. The *yoroidoshi* was very thick with a triangular blade, designed for piercing armor. The *kubikiri*, meaning "head cutter," has its cutting edge on the inside of the curve. It is probable that the *kubikiri* was carried by high ranking samurai who had the honor of removing the heads of slain enemies as trophies. The fan *tanto* was a dagger which, when sheathed, looked like a fan. It was often used by women, monks, and retired samurai as a concealed weapon. *Tessen* ("fans") were effective weapons in their own right (*see page 144*).

TESSEN

In addition to their swords, the samurai carried specialized concealed weapons such as the *tessen*, or fan. These could be used when a samurai was otherwise unarmed, such as indoors when swords would be left at the door.

The samurai customarily carried the *tessen* in his hands or tucked into his belt (*obi*). The *tessen* played an important role in Japanese etiquette, especially on formal occasions, hence many samurai carried one.

The forerunner of the *tessen* was the *gunbei-uchiwa*, which was a solid roundish fan used as a signaling device on the battlefield.

Tessen were constructed of iron and were either *menhari-gata* (a real folding fan with metal ribs that was expensive), or the more common *tenarashi-gata* (a non-folding solid bar of metal or wood in a fan shape).

The eight to ten metal ribs of the *menhari-gata* were covered with silk or highly lacquered strong paper (*washi*) treated with oil. Sometimes, bamboo ribs were included in the structure, making the *tessen* lighter and easier to carry.

There are many recorded accounts of duels won using a *tessen*, and even deaths. A famous sixteenth-century samurai, Ganryu, defeated several opponents simultaneously, armed only with a *tessen*.

It was considered bad form for a samurai to use his sword against an enemy of lower rank, but *tessen-jutsu* was considered to be a sophisticated alternative to swordplay.

MANRIKIGUSARI

The name of this weapon means "strength of a thousand men." It consists of a short length of metal chain, about two to three feet long, with weights on each end. It could be used to parry blows from swords, sticks, and polearms, and was highly effective at entangling a weapon and then disarming an opponent. The chain could also be used to restrain an attacker once he was subdued. *Manrikigusari* could easily be concealed, and when swung with force and deadly accuracy the weights could break a bone or crack the skull. It was supposedly developed in the late 1700s by a samurai named Masaki Dannoshin Toshimitsu as a way to kill without bloodshed. Bloodless killing was important because spilling blood on palace grounds and other sacred places was sacrilegious. Masaki was head sentry at the main gate of Edo-jo (Tokyo castle) where even drawing a sword within the castle was forbidden.

SHAKUHACHI

The most unlikely samurai defensive weapon is a bamboo flute called a *shakuhachi*. Originally, this end-blown flute was used solely as a musical instrument, and was constructed from the middle section of a bamboo culm. It was made popular by the Buddhist Fuke sect during the thirteenth century as an alternative to sutra chanting. However, during the sixteenth century, large numbers of samurai joined groups of itinerant preachers who were known as the *komuso* ("priests of nothingness"). They walked from village to village, wearing large baskets over their heads to symbolize their worldly detachment, playing the flute, preaching their doctrine of emptiness, and receiving alms. During the sixteenth century, the *komusu* spied on other samurai to protect the shogun from possible rebellion and were granted sole right to play the instrument in return. By now, their flutes were made from the spiked root section of the bamboo, so they could be used as a ferocious clubbing weapon.

KANSASHI

Women from samurai families were often trained to defend themselves, and a hairpin called a *kansashi* was their weapon of last resort. These pins were about six-inches long and used to keep the hair up and in place, but in an emergency they were an effective stabbing weapon strong enough to pierce an attacker's chest or throat.

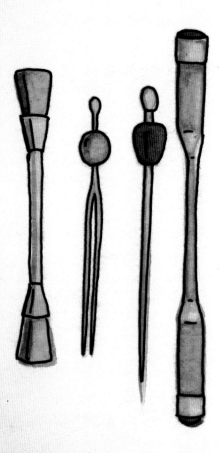

ARQUEBUS

This early gun became one of the samurai's most important weapons in the second half of the sixteenth century. The Japanese had been familiar with Chinese handguns since 1510, but the more sophisticated arquebus was introduced into Japan by shipwrecked Portuguese traders in 1543. Shimazu Takahisa was the first samurai general to use the arquebus in battle when attacking the fortress of Kajiki in the Osumi province. Soon, Japanese swordsmiths were mass-producing these next-generation weapons, and by the 1550s they were a common sight on the battlefield.

Unlike their European counterparts, Japanese arquebuses were manufactured with a more limited range of bores, so bullets were easier to mass produce and Japanese soldiers could be equipped with a large amount of ammunition.

The arquebus's main advantage was that it took much less training and little strength to use, compared to the years of expertise required to use a longbow effectively. It could also be fired from the shoulder, unlike the heavier musket which had to be mounted on a rest. However, it did have certain drawbacks. It took a long time to reload and fire (about twenty seconds for a good marksman), and did not have the range or accuracy of a bow and arrow. Also, it was subject to the whims of the weather: when it rained, the fuse got wet and the gun wouldn't fire. Although the fuses were boiled in chemicals to make them burn more easily, and a small box was fitted over the touch hole to shelter them, fuses were always vulnerable to the rain.

CANNON

The Sengoku period saw the appearance of the cannon. The Japanese did not find cannon production easy, in marked contrast to how they innovated and developed European firearms such as the arquebus. A limited number of cannons were manufactured in Nagasaki, but the Japanese seemed to prefer European cannons, which they acquired from European traders.

Previously, when the Japanese lost a battle owing to their enemy's new weapons or superior tactics, they usually responded to the defeat by developing their own versions of these weapons, or by changing their tactics. This did not happen with the cannon, despite the devastating attack on Moji castle by Portuguese cannon, in 1561. When the Japanese invaded Korea in 1592, they did not take any cannons with them. Initially, they took many Korean castles with arquebus fire, but later they were attacked by Chinese and Korean cannons. They responded by using cannons captured from the Koreans and mounting them from a few coastal fortresses, but cannons were still very few in number.

Many of the cannons were acquired from the West, but they had limited tactical use on the battlefield, because of their lack of mobility and occasionally due to the weather: they were present at the battle of Sekigahara in September 1600, but weren't used because of the rain.

However, cannons were effective during castle sieges where they were an effective psychological weapon rather than a weapon of mass destruction. For example, during the Osaka Winter Campaign, Tokugawa Ieyasu trained a hundred cannons at the keep of the castle to scare the inhabitants to come to terms.

Imagawa Yoshimoto

1519-1560

Originally planning to become a monk, Imagawa Yoshimoto instead became the *daimyo* of the Suruga and Totomi provinces—and ultimately the Mikawa province—until 1560. That year, his over-confidence led to his own demise, and the beginning of the end of the Imagawa line.

Imagawa Kazusa no suke Ujichika (1473-1526), Yoshimoto's father, sent him to the Zentokuji temple in Suruga where Yoshimoto studied to become a monk. Ujiteru, the eldest son of Ujichika, came to power in 1526, but died ten years later, setting off a battle for succession between his two brothers. Seeing an opportunity, Yoshimoto left Zentokuji and outfought both siblings to gain control. In a move that foreshadowed Yoshimoto's soon-to-be known diplomatic skills, he married Takeda Nobutora's sister the following year, thereby forming an alliance with the powerful Takeda clan. His troops helped Takeda Shingen conquer the Kai province in 1540, solidifying their relationship. Yoshimoto helped the Takeda against the Hojo in 1544, and when the fighting reached a stalemate he negotiated a peace treaty at Kitsunebashi.

In addition to his diplomatic skills, Yoshimoto was a good civic administrator. He was responsible for initiating land surveys and for creating a cultural center at Sumpu. His managerial acumen helped him bring together factions of the Imagawa and expand his area of power and influence. With the assistance of his uncle, Sessai Choro—who was also known as Taigen Sessai—Yoshimoto conquered the Totomi and the Matsudaira.

今川義元

In 1545, Yoshimoto put together an alliance between the Takeda, Hojo, and Imagawa. His diplomatic skills were held in such high regard that Hojo Ujiyasu asked him to intercede with Takeda Shingen, requesting that the Takeda forebear from attacking Kozuke because the Hojo had plans to invade.

By 1560, Yoshimoto called up more than 15,000 soldiers from Suruga and Mikawa to attack Oda Nobunaga at Kyoto. He was successful en route, destroying Nobunaga's forts at Marume and Terabe. Yoshimoto ordered his troops to rest in the Dengakuhazama, but Nobunaga had plans of his own. Nobunaga's soldiers were able to sneak up on an overly confident Yoshimoto's camp, attacking after a violent thunderstorm. Mori Shinnosuke killed Yoshimoto in the ensuing battle and the Imagawa troops fled.

Yoshimoto was succeeded by Ujizane, who was defeated in 1569 by the Takeda and Tokugawa clans, bringing an end to the Imagawa line.

Miyamoto Musashi

1584–1645

Miyamoto Musashi was one of the most skilled swordsmen in history. He was most likely born into a samurai family called the Hirata in the village of Miyamoto in present-day Mimasaka. His family owed allegiance to the Shinmen clan. From the age of seven he was raised by his uncle as a Buddhist in Shoreian temple, near to Hirafuku. It is said that in his infancy he suffered from a skin complaint, believed to be eczema, which caused him to have a pock-marked complexion in adulthood.

His warrior name is thought to have been taken from a warrior monk named Musashibo Benkei, who served under Minamoto no Yoshitsune.

When he was thirteen he defeated his first opponent, a sword adept of the Shinto-ryu style named Arima Kihei. Then, at sixteen, he defeated a powerful master named Akiyama of Tajima province.

In 1600, he took part on the side of Toyotomi against the Tokugawa, and was involved in the assault of Fushimi castle, the defense of Gifu castle, and the famed Battle of Sekigahara.

At the age of twenty-one, he came to Kyoto and challenged the Yoshioka School of swordsmanship. Then, he spent the next seven years traveling around Japan on a warrior pilgrimage, honing his skills.

宮本 武蔵

His most famous duel was against his most challenging opponent, Sasaki Kojiro, who had developed a new sword technique based on the movements of a swallow's tail in flight. Musashi heard of Kojiro's fame and asked Lord Hosokawa, through one of his retainers, Nagaoka Sado Okinaga, for permission to fight. The date was set at 8:00 A.M. on April 13, 1612, on the remote island of Funajima. Musashi arrived over three hours late, to unsettle his opponent. Kojiro attacked first (with a *nodachi*) after being taunted by Musashi, who killed him with a single strike to the head with a wooden sword he had made by paring down one of his oars. He then escaped in his boat. After this duel he stopped using real swords, so great were his fighting skills. Some scholars believe that Kojiro's death was a politically-motivated assassination by Musashi and his followers, and that Musashi cheated.

The rest of his life has passed into Japanese legend; he won over sixty duels without being defeated once. Some scholars have argued that he defended Osaka Castle and helped to put down the Shimabara Rebellion of 1638.

He founded the Hyoho Ni To Ichi Ryu style of swordsmanship and in the year of his death completed a book on strategy and philosophy, *Go Rin No Sho (The Book of the Five Rings),* which is still studied by martial artists and business people today.

CHAPTER 5
Samurai at War

During wartime a samurai warrior had the opportunity to channel all his peacetime daily preparation into battle, his very reason for living. Now he had the chance to demonstrate his skills and make a name for himself as a fearsome and honorable warrior.

When the call to arms came, a full-time samurai would switch from guard duty to campaign duty; if the samurai were part-time, as was common before the Separation Edict (*see page 35*), he would have to rush from the rice fields and change into battle dress, much like a modern-day volunteer firefighter would.

During times of war the samurai were mobilized into a hierarchical fighting unit. The *daimyo*'s closest retainers became his office corps, and an elite corps of samurai warriors formed a group called *umamawari*, or "horse guards."

The *umamawari* dressed differently than the regular samurai. For example, Oda Nobunaga's *umamawari* wore red or black *horo* on their backs. In times of peace they would form an elite bodyguard for the *daimyo*; at war they would lead the attack.

Some part-time samurai actually kept their armor with them in the fields. For instance, the farmer-samurai of Chosokabe Motochika kept their armor in boxes by the side of the paddy field and their spears stuck in the ground nearby. This motley crew were known as the *ichiryo gusoku*, or "owners of one suit of armor." A richer and more powerful *daimyo* such as Hideyoshi would have a much more intricate system of mobilizing his forces, so that his samurai would be supported by a back-up crew of laborers and boatmen and other attendants that outnumbered the actual fighting men.

However, it was preferable for a samurai to make careful preparations for battle, including bathing and perfuming himself before putting on his armor. Many warriors even placed incense inside their helmet so that if they were decapitated their heads would make a sweet-smelling trophy.

Before the assembled army began to march, the samurai faced an inspection. In some circumstances, a poor performance at muster was punishable by death. Before the advance to Odawara in 1590, the *daimyo* Gamo Ujisato inspected his troops and cut off a man's head for being out of line, then dispassionately offered his fine helmet to another soldier.

There were many rituals to perform before leaving for battle, including praying for victory to powerful gods such as *Fudo*, "the immoveable one." Buddhist priests chanted prayers or wrote them on wooden sticks called *goma*, which were then burned. A samurai victory prayer usually included a list of how his side had been wronged by the enemy.

The final ritual consisted of a farewell meal of *kachi guri* ("victory chestnuts"), *kombu* ("seaweed"), and *awabi* (a sea snail delicacy). There would be no luxuries while samurai were on the march, so this lucky banquet was savored.

The order to march came from the *daimyo*, who would make the cry of "*Ei! Ei!*" to which the samurai response was always, "*O!*"

Scouts and Messengers

Scouts were an essential component for effective communications. They would ride on ahead of a marching army and bring back vital intelligence about what the enemy was doing. By necessity these men were some of the most skilled riders in the army, and sometimes they would engage the enemy in small skirmishes to test their capability and spirit. Scouts were also used to hand-deliver important messages to the *daimyo*.

In one famous incident at Kangui in 1593, Kuroda Nagamasa sent five men to the castle with the message: "Critical alert. The enemy has crossed the river during the night and are setting up lines on our side. We expect to engage them in battle soon. Please send reinforcements immediately." However, Awayama Shiro'emon, who had just arrived to take command, realized that the castle was too far away for the reinforcements to arrive in time. He crossed out the final sentence, and replaced it with three words acknowledging their fate: "Rest in peace."

During battle, members of an elite messenger corps called the *tsukai-ban* were used to deliver messages and pass on orders between friendly troops. It was important that they could be easily recognized in the heat of battle, so they wore extra large *sashimono* on their helmets. Takeda Shingen's messengers wore a *sashimono* with a picture of a busy centipede.

Messengers also used a *horo*, a brightly-colored cloak bearing the *daimyo*'s *mon* ("badge") stretched over a wicker frame. As the messenger rode, the *horo* puffed up with air so that he could be seen from a distance.

THE BATTLE BEGINS

Once the army reached the site of the battle, if it had been prearranged (rather than being an ambush), it wasn't unusual to see crowds of onlookers watching the spectacle from a safe vantage point, out of range of the weapons. When Tachibana Muneshige attacked Otsu castle in 1600, the nearby slopes of Mount Hiei were crowded with picnicking spectators.

The samurai prepared themselves mentally for battle by Zen meditation and focused concentration.

Being the first samurai into battle was a great honor. Competition to make the first strike was fierce. At the battle of Uji in 1184, two samurai rode head to head across a river to be the first into battle. In 1600 during the Sekigahara campaign, Tokugawa Ieyasu instructed two elite warriors to jointly lead an advance on Gifu castle. It was agreed beforehand that Ikeda Terumasa and Fukushima Masanori would approach in unison, but they ended up arguing about who should be first and on the eve of the battle Masanori challenged Terumasa to a duel. Finally, they agreed to attack the front and rear of the castle simultaneously, but their squabbling lost them valuable time and, with it, the element of surprise.

BATTLE TACTICS

Tactics developed slowly over the course of samurai history. In the early days, an infantry squad of mounted samurai conscripts fought each other traditionally in small supporting groups. The Mongol invasions with phalanxes of fighters were a complete shock to the conscripts. Instead of changing their tactics, they reverted back to their old ways after the *kamikaze* ("divine wind") destroyed the Mongol fleet.

The conscript system was later abolished and the mounted archers dominated the battlefield, with the *ashigaru* relegated to a more inferior role. As the centuries passed, samurai increasingly saw them as their inferiors.

In early times there were set piece battles, beginning with the firing of signal arrows that invoked the *kami* to witness their battle exploits, followed by a duel of arrows intended to exercise the samurai "Way of the Bow and Horse." After the set piece battles, which would have a high body count, there followed duels called *ikkiuchi* ("single-mounted conflict") between selected samurai warriors, prefaced by lengthy genealogical declarations.

However, there were plenty of skirmishes that were not planned. Ambushes and guerrilla tactics were not incompatible with the samurai code, and there are many examples in the war chronicles of men, women, and children being slaughtered in surprise raids. The words of heroic samurai Minamoto Tametomo demonstrate that brutal tactics lived side by side with more formal military encounters:

"According to my experience, there is nothing so advantageous in striking down enemies as a night attack. . . If we set fire to three sides and secure the fourth, those fleeing the flames will be struck down by

arrows, and for those who seek to avoid the arrows, there will be no escape from the flames."

Taking the head of a slain enemy was a great accolade. Even in the confusion of the battlefield, the fierce competition between one's samurai comrades to secure personal credit was paramount, as demonstrated by this account of Okochi Hidemoto's during the capture of Namwon in Korea:

"Okochi cut at the right groin of the enemy on horseback and he tumbled down. As his groin was excruciatingly painful from this one assault the enemy fell off on the left-hand side. There were some samurai standing nearby and three of them struck at the mounted enemy to take his head. Four men had now cut him down, but as his plan of attack had been that the abdominal cut would make him fall off on the left, Okochi came running round so that he would not be deprived of the head."

The fighting would become quite generalized after the initial archery volleys, and small, autonomous groups of samurai would seek out worthy opponents, rather than being directed from above by a single battle plan. There would be lots of pockets of fighting taking place all over the battlefield. Even with the overall battle lost, if the samurai had acquitted themselves well, individual reputations could be established. Sometimes, there was an uneasy marriage between individual glory and the needs of the group.

During the Nanbokucho Wars in the fourteenth century, fighting was focused on the besieging and defending of castle fortresses, with the occasional open

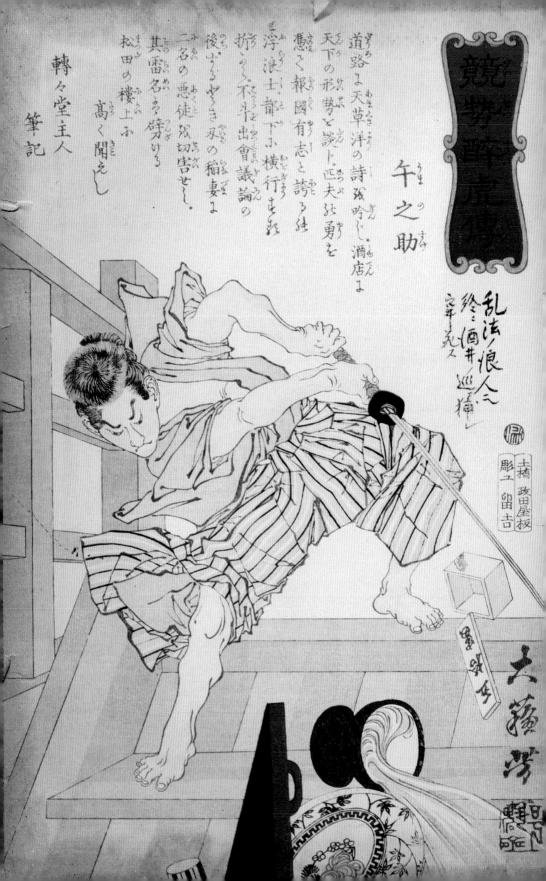

競勢酔虎傳

午之助

道路よ天草洋の詩強吟じ酒店よ
天下の形勢と誇ト匹夫が勇を
懸く報國有志と誇ら往
是浮浪士都下小横行きま其
捨りゞ不斗出會議論の
後じゐゞさゞき双の稲妻よ
二名の悪徒殘切害せし
其雷名を磅ける
松田の樓上ふ
高く聞えし

轉々堂主人
筆記

乱法ノ浪人ヌ
終ニ酒井巡獺
辛天ヌ

⑬

土橋 政田屋板
彫工 留吉

大蘇芳

battle such as Minatogawa, where traditional battle tactics were used. In siege situations, samurai fought mainly on foot and with less cumbersome armor.

During the Muromachi period (1333-1573), the use of mounted samurai warriors went into steep decline. With the increased reliance on lightly armored and highly mobile foot soldiers (*ashigaru*) using long bows, an individual mounted samurai was easily overcome by sheer numbers and hails of arrows.

The *ashigaru* of this period were well suited to guerrilla tactics, and the *daimyo* began to use them in raiding parties. For example, before the battle of Shijo Nawate, it says in the historical epic, the *Taiheiki*, "Sasaki Sado Hangwan Nyudo sent 2,000 horsemen up the mountain to the south of Ikoma . . . out of the men and horses 800 *shahu no ashigaru* ["foot soldier archers"] were launched, and fired prolifically at the horses of the enemy." This style of fighting became known as *nobushi* warfare, and for the first time samurai generals increasingly found themselves commanding infantry, rather than solely fighting for individual glory.

By now spears were being used extensively, with lines of infantry spear carriers fighting at the front of the battle. Later still, spears became the weapon of choice for the samurai, preferred over the bow and arrow.

It is in this period, with its emphasis on stealth tactics and secret intelligence gathering, assassination squads of specially trained martial artists, called *shinobi,* came into vogue. Today, these *shinobi* are more widely known by the popular term ninja. Contrary to a widespread misconception, ninja and samurai are not the same thing. The covert methods of the ninja were initially considered dishonorable by the samurai, as this passage from the *Shomonki* samurai war chronicle demonstrates:

"Over forty of the enemy were killed on that day, and only a handful managed to escape with their lives. Those who were able to survive the fighting fled in all directions, blessed by Heaven's good fortune. As for Yoshikane's spy Koharumaru, Heaven soon visited its punishment upon him: his misdeeds were found out, and he was captured and killed."

During the Period of the Warring States the *ashigaru* continued to grow in number and form armies. Originally, the *ashigaru* had been opportunist mercenaries who joined up for the spoils, but as the *daimyo* became more and more reliant on them, they had to be made more disciplined and be given greater incentives to remain loyal. Furthermore, the use of lines of long-shafted spear carriers demanded tighter discipline and training.

A successful samurai general now needed to be a tactician who could form alliances between smaller armies and then direct them in a synchronized strategic campaign. In the past, he would have led his troops into battle. Now, he stayed back, and from a vantage position passed his orders down the chain of command. This demanded coordination and an efficient communication system—all a far cry from the days past of individual glory. No longer was the signal arrow that initiated the battle shot by a high-ranking samurai at the head of his troops; now it was fired by a lowly *ashigaru*, to be followed by exchanges of arquebus fire prior to a charge of spear carriers.

The arquebus fire at the start of the battle was a deciding factor in the overall outcome, since an effective first strike could shock and disorient the *ashigaru* missile troops behind. Two ranks of arquebus fire seems to have been the norm, although Oda Nobunaga used three ranks at Nagashino.

Battles usually ended when one or both armies had had enough and retreated, often with no strategic gain on either side. Few battles were fought to the death. Even the five famous battles of Kawanakajima served little purpose other than to decimate both armies, so that when leaders Uesugi Kenshin and Takeda Shingen returned to their respective domains, Oda Nobunaga was able to exploit their weaknesses.

Some skirmishes were purely shows of strength, and a truce would be struck before the battle so that everyone could return home without fighting.

FLAGS AND EMBLEMS

The *Bushido Shoshinshu* of Taira Shigesuke stresses the importance of samurai keeping the "appropriate military equipment and weaponry corresponding to their status . . . such as the individual emblems, the helmet crests, the spear emblems, the sleeve emblems, and the carrier emblems—recognition emblems such as these must always be provided for the whole house." Identification on the battlefield was paramount: "those who are killed by their own allies because of neglecting recognition emblems have died for nothing."

The best-known Japanese heraldic devices were *mon* ("badges"), which were very simple and identified individual samurai families. The motifs were usually based on plants, heavenly bodies, and geometric designs. The color of the *mon* was not fixed, but it was usually contrasted against a light background, such as black or red on white.

Mon were often displayed had both standards above the peak of a samurai helmet, as well as being incorporated into scabbard designs or decorative motifs on clothing. However, they didn't always appear on battle flags.

During the Sengoku period, heraldry became very important, with extensive use of colored flags to represent units and sub-units of an army. From the second half of the sixteenth century, large numbers of *ashigaru* carried flags.

For example, in 1575, Uesugi Kenshin had more flag carrying footsoldiers than arquebus troops: they comprised nearly six percent of the total army.

One of the most important roles on the battlefield was the post of *hata bugyo* ("flag chief") to ensure that all the flags were displayed correctly.

The most common flags were *hata jirushi* ("streamers"); in later centuries *nobori*, long vertical flags held rigid by a short cross-pole, became popular. They were carried in a leather cup attached to the flag bearer's belt, or on a *sashimono* holder worn on the back of the armor.

The *sashimono* was an important heraldic innovation during the Sengoku period. It consisted of a small flag held rigid by two lacquered poles attached to the back of the armor. This was held in place by a rope which went under the armpits and secured to the breastplate with metal rings. A *sashimono* could get in the way during close combat: a silk screen of the Summer Campaign of Osaka in Hikone castle shows an attendant holding his master's *sashimono* while he is fighting.

The *daimyo*'s insignia was the most impressive of all. His massive flags were known as *uma jirushi* (literally "horse insignia") of which there were an *o-uma jirushi* ("great standard") and a *ko-uma jirushi* ("lesser standard"). Many were huge three-dimensional objects such as kites, gongs, or umbrellas. Wealthier *daimyo* had both standards, while lesser *daimyo* settled for just one. In 1645, the Tokugawa shogunate declared that a *daimyo* with an income above 1,300 *koku* could have a lesser standard, and a great standard as well if he earned more than 6,000 *koku*.

In 1650, a monk named Kyuan completed an illustrated book of nearly all of the samurai insignia of the Sengoku period called *O-Uma Jirushi*, which still survives today.

SHELLS, BELLS, DRUMS, GONGS, AND CLAPPERS

The oldest and most traditional method of audible signaling on the battlefield and on the march was a large conch shell called a *jinkai*. It was carried by the *kaiyaku* ("trumpeter") in a cord basket and was played through a brass mouthpiece.

The most skilled conch players were the *yamabushi*, the mountain-dwelling followers of the religious sect of Shugendo. Many conscripts were recruited by *daimyo* for their conch-playing expertise.

The *jinkai*'s main strength as an instrument was its strident clarion call, which could be heard above the din of battle and also contained an epic heroic quality in its tone. However, it was also used for signaling and there was an established code of conch-calls which every soldier was expected to recognize.

An army began marching after three sets of blasts from the conch shell. The first set of calls was nine notes played three times in a row; it warned soldiers to finish eating. The second call, nine notes played nine times in a row, instructed the soldier to be ready to leave. The third call, nine notes played twenty-seven times in a row, was the signal to march. The patterns of the conch blowing also had a religious significance: the final calls followed the rhythm of a Buddhist chant.

The conch was also blown at two-hour intervals during the night to mark time, and additional time-calling blasts were made during the day. When an army advanced at night, its departure was preceded by seven conch blows.

A weakening enemy could expect to hear the most sinister conch call of all: seven sets of seven blasts, followed by five sets of five, three sets of three, and a

final long blast. This signal instructed the advancing army to wipe out its opponents.

Drums were used from very early on in Japanese military history. War drums, which were large and highly decorated, were supported on a strong wooden framework, or else they were carried on a pole by two men. They were used to dictate marching pace, lift an army's morale, and mark time. In a castle, the drum was situated at the top of a drum tower.

A *taiko yaku* ("drummer") set the pace for a marching army, with soldiers taking six paces between each beat. By the Warring States period, there was a well-established drum language of commands. The *Gunji Yoshu* war chronicle gives these instructions about drum calls: "To summon one's allies the drum call is nine sets of five beats at an appropriate pace, and when advancing one's own troops and pursuing an enemy the call is nine sets of three beats, speeding up three or four times, and the giving of the war cry. As for the number of war cries, shout '*Ei! Ei! O!*' twice."

Although bells were less mobile than drums and conch shells, their sound carried well, and a static bell mounted in a *daimyo's* headquarters could be used to signal and encourage his troops. The Uesugi family used a bell like a conch shell, to prepare the army for battle, only with single peals rather than a complex system of blasts. However, usually the signal to advance or retreat was made by portable drums.

Gongs (*dora*) and wooden clappers (*hyoshigi*) had a limited audible range on the battlefield, but they were used for timekeeping in cities during the Edo period and in army camps during the Warring States period.

CASTLE WARFARE

According to F. W. Seal, "many Sengoku battles were fought near forts, which were often the prize involved in these struggles." The capture of castles "was often the primary goal of military operations and acted as a measuring stick of success. The Mori's long war against the Amako of Izumo, for example, was essentially a string of fort captures that culminated in the final siege of Gassan-Toda, which fell in January 1566. This tended to make for very long 'wars.' The Shimazu and Ito were actively at odds for decades, while the Hojo and Satomi fought off and on for nearly sixty years."

Because wood was abundant and stone was not, until the late sixteenth century, Japanese castles were very simple wooden edifices built into the contours of a mountain or linking a number of hills. Gates were linked by wooden stockades, and the hills were actually sculpted to produce several interlocking baileys. Little stone was used in these castles until the late sixteenth century. Initially, stone was only used to strengthen foundations and to shore up earthworks. Later, the walls inside the castle were made out of wattle and daub, which was plastered to make them more fire-resistant. The curving roofs were tiled for waterproofing.

The stone foundations provided some protection against earthquakes, but they were easy to scale, so the castle walls were filled with secret holes and trapdoors through which rocks and boiling water could be poured. Slits in the walls for arrows and guns were also common features.

The inside of the castle was subdivided into a maze of rooms, courtyards, and corridors to confuse invaders and to make it easier to trap them within a system of gates.

A castle network was common, with many subordinate castles branching out from a single main castle called a *honjo*, which housed the *daimyo*. The castles would communicate with each other by a chain of fire signals. The mountain was then cut into to provide level ground to accommodate the barracks. When the cutaway slopes began to be reinforced with tightly packed stones, they could support heavier and stronger walls.

There are numerous accounts of castle sieges in samurai history of the sixteenth century. The element of surprise in attack was always important. During the siege of Un no Kuchi in 1536, Takeda Shingen marched through thick snow to launch a victorious surprise assault. However, after 1570, when stone bases became popular fortifications, some sieges lasted several years, most notably the fortress cathedral of Ishiyama Homganji. Its inhabitants, the *Ikko-ikki*, were besieged by Oda Nobunaga for ten years. Other castles fell several times in a short time: the castle of Moji, which overlooks the straits of Shimonoseki, was conquered five times in four years.

The arquebus became an important castle siege weapon. In 1549, shortly after they had been introduced by the Portuguese, arquebuses were used to capture Kajiki Castle in the south of the country. Five years later, Oda Nobunaga effectively deployed rotating volleys from arquebuses across the moat against Muraki Castle, a tactic that became popular in many subsequent castle sieges.

Brutal psychological warfare was frequently used to weaken the resolve of castle dwellers. During the siege of Shika in 1547, Takeda Shingen displayed the severed heads of his enemy in front of the castle walls. Conversely, besieged castle inhabitants sometimes bluffed the enemy with a show of false strength. When Takeda Shingen attacked the mountain castle of Katsurayama, he was unaware that its greatest weakness was that there was no water supply inside. All the water had to be carried from the lower slopes, from a well near the Joshoji temple. However, the Ochiai soldiers inside the castle had plentiful supplies of rice, so they decided to pour it over the walls, fooling the enemy into thinking

it was water. The trick would have worked had not the chief priest of the temple betrayed them by revealing their secret weakness to the Takeda.

After that, Takeda Shingen captured the well and set fire to the castle, resulting in the mass suicide of hundreds of women and children who threw themselves from the battlements. The castle burned to ashes and legend tells that anyone digging in the site can still find charred rice.

Sieges didn't always end in mass suicide or slaughter. Often, if the castle didn't receive reinforcements, those inside simply switched sides and joined the besieging force. The Moris changed sides twice (from Ouchi to Amako, and then back again) when they recognized that defeat was inevitable. Conversely, if the inhabitants of a castle had plenty of supplies, they could hold out until the besieging army ran out of supplies and went home.

Another good example of the psychological aspect of castle warfare occurred during the siege of Minowa in 1566. The castle was defended by Nagano Narimasa, whose fearsome reputation discouraged attackers. For this reason, when he died in 1561 his followers kept his death a secret, even after his heir Narimori became the new leader. Their enemy, the Takeda, soon uncovered the deception, and killed Narimori.

In 1581, invaders used starvation on a scale not seen before in Japanese castle warfare as a tactic against Kikkawa Tsuneie at Tottori. The castle dwellers held out for 200 days, until faced with a choice of eating each other or surrender. They chose the latter.

During sieges, written messages were sent over the walls of the castle by means of letters attached to arrows. This method of communication was used frequently during the siege of Hara castle in 1638.

WOUNDS AND TAKING OF HEADS

A samurai rarely died by decapitation, but was more likely to bleed to death from his many wounds. While *katana* swords have a fearsome reputation, duels usually resulted in several cuts rather than a single decisive killing stroke. Death from arrows was also common, and there are many Japanese silk paintings showing warriors still fighting with numerous arrows sticking into them.

Medical treatment was basic and, in many cases, unavailable. Minor cuts were often treated with a coagulant called *yomogi* (mugwort). One remedy included placing dried feces over the wound, then using mulberry root sutures to close the skin, followed by a sprinkling of cat-tail pollen. According to the *Hagakure*, therapeutic consumption of horse feces was also practiced: Amari Tozo ordered one of his wounded samurai to drink a solution of water and the dung of a red-haired horse, and he even set the warrior a good example by drinking some himself.

Head collection was an important samurai tradition. After a battle, hundreds of heads would be piled up by both sides in the commanders' headquarters. Sometimes there would be an exchange of heads between sides.

Before being presented to the *daimyo*, the heads were cleaned and their hair was combed before being inspected, usually by samurai women. This practice is described by Yamada Kyoreki's daughter, Oan:

"My mother and I, as well as the wives and daughters of the other retainers, were in the castle's keep casting bullets. Severed heads taken by our allies were also gathered up in this area of the [Mino] castle. We attached a tag to each head in order to identify them properly. Then we repeatedly blackened their teeth. Why did we do that? A long time ago, blackened teeth were admired as the sign of a distinguished man."

The black dye she used for this procedure was called *ohaguro*. The whole process must have been very desensitizing. In an earlier passage she said, "I did not even have a sense of being alive—all I could feel was fear and terror." Later she said "Even these severed heads no longer held any terror for me. I used to sleep enveloped by the bloody odor of those old heads."

The fact that the samurai cleaned the heads of their enemies shows that they had respect for the fallen warriors, but mostly it was to prepare them for presentation to the *daimyo*.

The importance of head presentation is demonstrated by an incident which took place at Oda Nobunaga's New Year's banquet in 1574. The highlight of the evening was the presentation of the heads of Asakura Yoshikaga, Asai Hisamasa, and Asai Nagmasa. Although the three high-status warriors had been killed the previous year, their heads had been preserved by layers of lacquer and gold dust.

It was important that the heads were attributed to the samurai who took them, so that an accurate record could be made. During the twelfth century when the quantity of heads taken mattered more than the reputation of the samurai from whom it had been taken, it was common practice for dead bodies to be decapitated on the battlefield. However, by the Sengoku period, this practice was frowned upon and it was only acceptable to behead a known, and high-status, personal kill.

The taking of an elite *tsukai-ban* messenger's head was a worthy prize, as this passage from *Hosokawa Yusai Oboegaki (The Diary of Hosokawa Yusai)* shows: "When taking the head of a *horo* warrior wrap it in the silk of the *horo*. In the case of an ordinary warrior, wrap it in the silk of the *sashimono*."

Taking heads during battle could, for obvious reasons, be a hindrance to victory. If a samurai bagged an important trophy, he often retired from the battlefield and took no further part in the fighting. Also, taking a head often attracted a swarm of enemy samurai ready to defend their fallen comrade's honor.

When Hojo Ujiyasu attacked Kawagoe castle in 1545, forbidding his men to take heads of enemies who greatly outnumbered them was one of the crucial factors in his success.

One solution to keep the samurai fighting was to allow heads to be taken and then discarded, provided that a samurai had reliable witnesses to the event. During the invasion of Korea, the shipping of hundreds of heads back to Toyotomi Hideyoshi was a logistical nightmare, so a gruesome compromise was reached. Only the heads of important generals were sent intact, accompanied by the ears and noses of the lesser fallen. At the height of the second invasion, barrel loads full of these facial features packed in brine were sent back to Hideyoshi. Many were buried in a mound in Kyoto to form a monument called the Mimizuka ("mound of ears") near Hideyoshi's Great Buddha. It is not known how many Korean soldiers and civilians were killed during the Korean invasions, but some estimates are as high as one million.

Kusunoki Masashige

1294-1336

Kusunoki Masashige was a modest landowner in Kwatchi province who responded to Emperor Go-Daigo's plea for military support against the Hojo in 1331. His first act, with 500 troops, was to secure a hilltop, where Prince Morinaga joined him.

The imperial cause seemed lost. Emperor Go-Daigo was imprisoned and Kusunoki and Prince Morinaga had no choice but to continue with the rebellion. In a three-week battle, the vastly outnumbered Masashige and his men defended Akasaka and Mt. Kongo. Although the *bakufu* forces cut off Kusunoki's water supply, he was determined to continue the fight. He ordered the castle torched and slipped out, tricking the Hojo into believing that he had committed suicide.

Kusunoki assembled another band of men the following year and began a campaign against *bakufu* forces in the Kinai while Prince Morinaga appealed to other landowners and warriors to rally against Kamakura.

In early 1333, sizable *bakufu* forces were sent against Chihaya, another Mt. Kongo fort defended by Kusunoki; Yoshino, headquarters of Prince Morinaga; and Akasaka, now under the control of Hirano Shogen. Akasaka and Yoshino fell quickly, but Kusunoki had had time to prepare Chihaya for a prolonged battle. Using everything from boiling water to rolling logs, Kusunoki held off the assault until Takauji and his army marched into Kyoto and occupied the city in the name of the emperor.

楠木正成

Peace was short-lived. By 1336, Takauji had split from the imperial cause and Nitta Yoshisada had become Go-Daigo's top commander. Nitta sent a messenger calling for Kusunoki to join the loyalist army, but Kusunoki objected to a confrontation with Takauji. Ever loyal to the emperor, however, Masashige raised troops for an army he believed doomed. Before he left, Masashige urged his eleven-year-old son, Masatsura, to remain brave and loyal to the emperor, a moment often depicted in Japanese art.

Kusunoki's men were set up on the west bank of the Minatogawa River, with his flank secured to the south by Nitta on the eastern side of the river. When the fighting started, Shoni attacked Nitta's front while Hosokawa sailed up to attack the rear. Nitta pulled back, leaving Kusunoki's 700 men to face Ashikaga Tadayoshi's army. After a six-hour battle, Masashige and his brother Masasue committed suicide, joined by those Kusunoki retainers who had not already been killed.

After the Meiji Restoration, Kusunoki Masashige became a national symbol: a samurai loyal to the emperor to his death. He was a useful symbol to a restored imperial court that had to reconcile its relationship with the samurai.

Minamoto Yoshitsune

1159-1189

"Yoshitsune has left great achievements; about this there is nothing to argue."

So begins an 1185 diary entry by Kujo Kanezane, a supporter of Yoshitsune's brother and, ultimately enemy, Yoritomo.

"In bravery, benevolence, and justice, he is bound to leave a great name to posterity. In this he can only be admired and praised," wrote Kenzane.

Yoshitsune's suicide guaranteed him an honorable place in history, while assuring his brother Yoritomo's memory would always be tarnished.

Minamoto Yoshitsune's father, Minamoto Yoshitomo, attempted to defy the Taira in 1159 but failed. He was assassinated a year later. Taira Kiyomori spared Yoshimoto's wife and children; Yoritomo was sent to Izu while Yoshitsune was sent to a temple north of Kyoto.

Yoritomo and Yoshitsune were reunited about twenty years later when Prince Mochihito called for the Minamoto to rise up against the Taira. In 1183, Yoshinaka, a Minamoto clan member, defeated the Taira at Kurikara and went on to occupy Kyoto. Against Yoritomo's wishes, Yoshinaka then tried to take full control of the Minamoto. Yoritomo sent Yoshitsune to rid Kyoto of his brother, Yoshinaka.

In 1184, Yoshitsune, now a general, led an army that included his brother Noriyori and Kajiwara Kagetoki into Kyoto.

源 義 経

Yoshinaka responded by placing troops at the Uji and Seta bridges on the Uji River, but Yoshitsune's army split and defeated Yoshinaka's men at both points. Yoshinaka tried to escape with some retainers, but he was trapped at Awazu and committed suicide.

With the emperor's support, Yoritomo sent Yoshitsune and Noriyori against the Taira. At Ichi no Tani, a fort covered from the rear by a steep incline, Yoshitsune launched a nighttime attack that brought the fort down. Yoshitsune then sent 7,000 men under Doi Sanehira's command to the western side of Ichi no Tani, while he led the remaining 3,000 men under his command to the cliffs above the fort. With the Taira's attentions on Doi and Noriyori, Yoshitsune led his men down the cliffs into the rear of the fort. Shocked by what they thought was impossible, the Taira panicked and retreated to their ships, which were anchored off shore.

Immediately after Ichi no Tani, Yoshitsune returned to Kyoto and served as Yoritomo's deputy until 1185. It was during that time that a rift between Yoshitsune and Yoritomo became evident. Yoshitsune went on to defeat the Taira at Yashima, arriving by ship and tricking them into believing he had many more troops that he did. As the Taira left their fort to fight, Yoshitsune's men were able to set the structure on fire. Yoshitsune pursued the fleeing Taira, culminating in a huge sea battle that the Minamoto won in less than a day. With the victory, the Taira clan was eliminated as a threat to the Minamoto.

Yoritomo, however, ordered Yoshitsune's death in 1189. Yoshitsune was in Koromogawa when Fujiwara Yasuhira attacked on Yoritomo's orders. Yoshitsune's old friend Benkei held off the attackers long enough for Yoshitsune to kill his young wife and commit suicide.

The Meiji Restoration, which took place between 1864 and 1868, saw the Tokugawa shogunate finally deposed, beginning a process of modernization in which Japan reforged links with other countries. It was the catalyst towards industrialization that led to the rise of Japan as a military power under the slogan of "National Wealth and Military Strength."

It also marked the end of the samurai. In 1871, with all the Tokugawa land already under control of the Meiji oligarchy, the *daimyo* were summoned before the Emperor and informed that their lands would return to him. About three hundred *daimyo*-controlled *han* ("domains") became prefectures under the control of a state-appointed governor. Many of them subsequently merged so that about seventy-five remained.

There were nearly two million samurai in Japan, all on a fixed stipend from the state. In 1873, they became subject to taxation, and three years later the samurai were obliged to turn their stipends into government bonds. Conscription was reintroduced, with every male serving three years in the army from the age of twenty-one. The samurai's privileged position as the only class permitted to carry arms had finally ended.

Epilogue

My own vows are the following:

Never to be outdone in the Way of the Samurai.

To be of good use to the master.

To be filial to my parents.

To manifest great compassion, and to act for the sake of Man.

If one dedicates these four vows to the gods and Buddhas every morning, he will have the strength of two men and will never slip backward. One must edge forward like the inchworm, bit by bit.

The gods and Buddhas, too, first started with a vow.

— *Hagakure*, Yamamoto Tsunetomo, (1659-1719)

Glossary

agemaki decorative knotted tassel

ashigaru foot soldier

awabi sea snail prized for its unique flavor

biwa short-necked fretted lute

bokuto wooden saber usually the size of a *katana*

botangake *wakabiki* armpit protectors with buttons

bushido "the Way of the Warrior"; the "code of honor" of the samurai class

chasen gami pigtail method of winding string round the lower half of the pigtail to make it stick out

chomage topknot

chu Confucian value of loyalty

daimyo feudal lord

daisho pairing of a *katana* and a *wakizashi*

do body part of a suit of armor

dora gongs

doshin samurai officers in the police force

eboshi cloth cap

ebu hollow part of a *yari* shaft

emishi indigenous people of Northern Honshu during the late Nara and early Heian periods

eriwa type of *nodowa* throat protector attached to the helmet with a buckle

fukigayeshi helmet winglets

fundoshi loincloth

futatsu-ori pigtail method in which the cylinder of hair is folded forward, and the front trimmed with a razor

genpuku rite in which a young samurai received his first adult haircut, sword, and suit of armor

geta clogs

goma prayer stick

gunbei-uchiwa signaling fan

gun'yakusho term used to describe a village that receives a tax break in return for providing men for military service

habiki sword with a blunt edge; also the practice of dulling a sword's blade so that it doesn't break

hachi bowl of a helmet

hachimaki headband

hachiwara "helmet breaker" sword

haidate thigh guards; apron-like pieces of cloth fringed with overlapping plates of metal

hakama loose samurai pants, worn over the *kimono*, paired with the *kataginu* to form a *kamishimo*

hamon pattern line between hard and soft metal on a sword blade

hanairo-odoshi light blue braid

hanamusubi flower-shaped knot

happuri head protector that guards the forehead and temples

haragei "belly performance"; mental and emotional concentration to focus the personal *ki* energy

haraidate socket on the peak of helmet for affixing crests

hata bugyo "flag commissioner"; senior samurai with responsibility for ensuring that all flags and standards are displayed according to an agreed battle plan

hata jirushi "streamers"; a type of flag

hikiawase place for tightening body armor, usually located on the right side

himo-tsuki *wakabiki* armpit protectors with cords

hishiniu lacing system of cross-knotting

hishinui-no-ita lowest row of a group of armor plates, so-called because it is often ornamented by a double row of crosslaces

hitatare two-piece costume worn by samurai before the Edo period

hoate "cheek protector"; armor mask covering the face from below eye level

hoko four-pronged samurai spear

honjo castle headquarters

horimono engraving; from the Japanese *horu* ("to carve") and *mono* ("thing")

horo brightly-colored cloak bearing a *daimyo*'s *mon*

hyoshigi wooden clappers

iai the ability to unsheathe the sword and deliver a fatal blow in one swift movement

inome small hole in the palm of a pair of gloves

inuoumono mounted archery involving shooting at dogs

iroiro-odoshi multi-colored lacing

ishizuki metal pommel

jinkai conch shell used for signaling

junshi "following in death"; the performance of *seppuku* following the death of one's master

jutte long iron truncheon used by feudal Japanese police officers

kabuto helmet

kachi guri "victory chestnuts"

kagemusha "shadow warrior"; decoy body-double used to protect an important general during battle

kaishakunin a "second" in *seppuku*

kaiyaku conch shell trumpeter

kamasu kissaki sword with chisel-shaped points

kami Shinto deity

kamikaze "divine wind"; the typhoon that destroyed the Mongol fleet in 1281

kamishimo two-piece costume worn over the *kimono*, consisting of a *kataginu* and a *hakama*

kansashi hairpin

kappa traditional straw raincoat worn by farmers

kare san-sui dry landscape gardens of raked gravel and stone

karo top-ranking samurai

kasa large straw hat

kata literally "form"; a detailed pattern of movements practiced in many Japanese arts

kataginu sleeveless jacket with large shoulders, paired with the *hakama* to form a *kamishimo*

katana curved, single-edged longsword

kate-bukuro provision bag

kawa-tabi tanned skin socks

kebiki odoshi closed space or full lacing with no gaps

keiko Japanese lamellar armor consisting of a sleeveless coat of plates and a flared thigh-length skirt

ki an invisible intrinsic life energy present inside the body of all living things

kiahan gaiters

kissaki sword tip, of which there are varying lengths and shapes

ko Confucian value of filial piety

kofun earthwork tombs of the Yamamoto rulers of ancient Japan

kohaze-gake *wakabiki* armpit protectors with hooks

koku unit of volume, originally defined as the amount of rice that could feed one person for a year, equivalent to forty-eight U.S. gallons

kombu type of seaweed

komuso "priests of nothingness"; itinerant *shakuhachi* flute players

kondei "strong youth"; military units recruited from the landowner class from the eighth century A.D.

kon-odoshi navy blue braid

kozan defensive scales used in armor

kubibukuro bag for carrying the severed head of an enemy

kubikiri "head cutter"; type of tanto

kusazuri "grass rubber"; flared skirt of defensive plates which protects the lower body

kuwagata antlers

kyba no michi "the Way of the Bow and Horse"

kyubi no ita armor plate used with the *sendan no ita* to protect the underarm area

mabisashi the peak of a helmet

maedate the crest of a helmet

mamorigatana "protective sword" for the express purpose of self-defense

manjuwa neck and armpit protector worn with a *nodowa*

manrikigusari "strength of a thousand men"; short length of metal chain, about two to three feet long, with weights on each end

meguriwa type of *nodowa* throat protector attached to the helmet with hooks

mempo "face cheek" armor mask covering the whole face

menhari-gata real folding fan (see *tenarashi-gata*)

mitsu-ori pigtail method of forming the hair into a cylinder then bending it forward, back, and forward again before tying it in place

mittsu-kuwagata triple-antler

mochi yari short polearm

mogami do laced lamellar full body armor popular in the sixteenth century

momen-tabi cotton cloth socks

momi-tabi red silk socks

mon identifying family "badge"

motodori pigtail

mune non-cutting side of sword blade

musha shugyo "warrior pilgrimages"; in medieval Japan, accomplished by traveling the country and challenging other warriors to combat

nagabakama formal pants with extra long legs that cover the feet and trail behind the wearer

naginata spear with a wooden shaft and a stout single-edged blade, slightly curved

naginata-jutsu the martial art of the *naginata*

nobori "upward," long vertical flags held rigid by a short cross-pole

nodachi field sword with a very long blade, first used by samurai in the four-teenth century

nodowa throat protector

nuinobe do full body armor composed of large scales

obi belt

odoshi suspensory and decorative lacing of Japanese armor

odoshige lacing hair

ohaguro black dye

omi no yari long polearm

o-yoroi "great armor," which first appeared during the tenth century A.D. and saw widespread use during the twelfth century

oyumi siege crossbow

ronin "men of the waves"; masterless samurai

saihai signaling baton

sakayaki the shaved front part of a samurai's head

sankin kotai alternate attendance system, introduced by the Tokugawa shogunate, obligating feudal lords to divide their time between Edo and their provincial domain

sarubo "monkey cheek" armor mask that covers only the cheeks and chin

sashimono "little banner" or flag mounted to the back of the armor

saya scabbard

sendan no ita armor plate used with the *kyubi no ita* to protect the underarm area

Sengoku jidai Warring States period, which lasted from roughly the mid-fifteenth century to the early seventeenth century

sensei term used to show respect to a person who has achieved a certain level of mastery in a particular field, especially the martial arts

seppuku suicide by disembowelment; also called *hara kiri*

shahu no ashigaru foot soldier archers

shakuhachi end-blown bamboo flute

shibui hidden beauty expressed in profound, unassuming quiet feeling and simple restraint

shikken regent of the shogun

shikoro neck guard

shinai pole made out of light bamboo

shingane iron core of a sword

shinobi secret intelligence gathering or assassination squads, more widely known by the popular term ninja

shinogi middle ridgeline of a sword

shitagarami individual lacing of armor plates

shogi martial art of Japanese chess, played on a grid of rectangles comprising nine rows and nine columns

shoji sliding room divider or door made of translucent paper

so-byakusho "ordinary" peasants

sode shoulder plates

sokotsu-shi atoning suicide

suburi sword drilling method involving swinging the sword over and over again at an imaginary opponent

sugake odoshi sparce-point lacing, in which pairs of braids are used

suji-bachi style of multi-plate helmet

suneate shin guards

tabi socks

tachi classic curved samurai sword predating the *katana*

taiko yaku drummer

tampo yari spear with a padded end

tanko "short armor"; the earliest form of Japanese armor

tanto dagger with usually single- or sometimes double-sided blade length of about six to twelve inches

tanto-jutsu martial art of the dagger

tatami "folded and piled" rectangular woven straw floor mats

tedate large mobile bamboo shield

tehen hole in the center of a helmet's crown

tenarashi-gata non-folding solid bar of metal or wood in a fan shape

tenugui white cotton cloth towel

tessen iron battle fan

tessen-jutsu martial art of the war fan

tokonoma decorative alcove in a Japanese home used for display; also the name of the room which contains the alcove

tosei gusoku "modern armor" used from the sixteenth to the nineteenth century

tsuba sword hand guard

tsubamegata "swallow pattern" armor mask that covers only the chin

tsukai-ban elite messenger corps

tsumeru sparring technique involving halting a strike a fraction of an inch before hitting its target

tsurubashiri leather panel covering the *do*

uagane outer zone cutting edge of a sword

uchi-bari padded inner cap of a helmet

uchi-bukuro money purse

uchi-gaye rice provision bag

udenuki safety cord to guard against dropping a sword

umamawari "horse guards"; elite corps of samurai

uma jirushi horse insignia

wakabiki armpit protectors

wakizashi traditional sword with a blade between twelve and twenty-four inches long, often used as a close-combat stabbing sidearm

waraji straw sandals

washi highly lacquered strong paper

watagami shoulder straps

yabusame martial art of mounted archery

yakiba wavy line indicating the boundary between the unhardened and hardened part of the blade

yamabushi mountain-dwelling followers of the religious sect of Shugendo

yari straight-headed polearm

yashiki mansion

yo-bukuro small storage pocket

yomogi "mugwort"; a plant used as a coagulant for minor wounds

yoroidoshi tanto with a thick triangular blade designed for piercing armor

yoroi-hitatare armor robe

yugake gloves

yukinoshita do full body armor characterized by large solid vertical plates around the torso and extensive lacquering

yumi longbow

zukuri a type of sword blade